Art of Work
The Art and Life of Haki R. Madhubuti

Lita Hooper

THIRD WORLD PRESS
CHICAGO

Third World Press
Publishers since 1967
Chicago

First Edition
Printed in the United States of America

12 11 10 09 08 07   5 4 3 2 1

Cover Design and Text Layout by Keir Thirus
Text set in Galliard and Fenice

Hooper, Lita.
  Art of work : the art and life of Haki R. Madhubuti/Lita Hooper.
— 1st ed.
       p. cm.
  Includes bibliographical references.
  ISBN 978-0-88378-255-2
  1. Madhubuti, Haki R., 1942- 2. Black Arts movement. I. Title.
  PS3563.A3397Z68 2007
  813'.54—dc22
  [B]
                                        2007010388

This book is dedicated to my children,
Malik Rasuli and Sojourner Imani.

I would like to thank my husband, Michael Simanga, for his encouragement and unbelievable support throughout the research and writing process for this book. I owe a special thanks to my mother, Charlie M. Hooper, and my father, Napoleon Hooper, who provided financial and spiritual support thoughout graduate school.

The staff at Third World Press were wonderful—particularly my editor, Gwendolyn Mitchell.

Last but certainly not least, I'd like to thank Haki Madhubuti, who graciously granted me access to his life and archives. Your life has been and continues to be a true work of art.

Contents

Introduction

I first met Haki R. Madhubuti at a poetry reading sponsored by the now defunct Guild Books in Chicago. He seemed to be hiding in a darkened corner near the stage as he listened to fellow poets. A fan of his work through borrowed copies of his early writings and anthologies, I watched him applaud each poet, known and unknown, who reached the microphone to participate in the marathon slam fundraiser. Modestly awaiting his introduction, he graciously shook the hands of the few young poets who recognized him. Then the slam ceased, everyone settled into their seats and the host introduced Madhubuti.

The applause was explosive as heads turned to see him walk onto the stage. At the microphone, he humbly thanked the audience and organizers for inviting him then he spoke briefly about the power and necessity of art in a violent and discouraging world. When he finished reading, the audience now on their feet, I knew one thing for certain: I would one day write about this man.

For years I replayed that night, ultimately deciding that Madhubuti would be the subject of my dissertation (should I ever make it to graduate school). This was fueled by my undergraduate experience at DePaul University, where I was introduced to literary theory. The English courses I took primarily focused on white writers; Black writers were often read at the end of the quarter—added as bonuses to a grueling eleven weeks of study. Fascinated by theoretical scholarship, I decided to someday focus on the literature of the Black Arts Movement, a movement that had been greatly under-appreciated in academia.

Even as an undergraduate student, I was surprised to learn that few scholars had seriously examined Madhubuti's contributions as a political activist and poet. In fact, very little had been written about him—an artist who had committed his life and work to the struggle for peace and justice. He was among the few outspoken activists and writers of his generation who had actually remained both optimistic and active after the Black Power Movement and Black Arts Movement of the 1960s and 1970s, continuing to blend art and activism, unlike many of his contemporaries. Undoubtedly, Haki Madhubuti is one of the most prolific writers to emerge from the Black Arts Movement, and his legacy deserves recognition.

This book is a result of my dissertation, which fulfilled a Doctor of Arts degree at Clark Atlanta University. In preparing the book, I simply wanted to give readers (those familiar and unfamiliar with Madhubuti's career) a close look at the man and his work. It is not intended to be a definitive study of Madhubuti, but rather a contribution toward much needed scholarship. Marlene Mosher's *New Directions from Don L. Lee* (1975) is certainly the most comprehensive examination of Madhubuti's poetry to date. Aside from magazine articles and short interviews, limited substantive text has been written on Madhubuti's extensive writing career.

In short, my intention was to write a book that offers future researchers some insight into the personal and professional choices he has made. To accomplish this, I have included a discussion of the evolution of his early poetry and essays. In addition, I offer the transcript of an interview I conducted with him in which he discusses the various roles he juggles—artist, scholar, activist, educator and entrepreneur—and the significant impact each has had on his art. For Madhubuti's life is an ongoing testament of his political consciousness and artistic convictions—both fundamental elements of the Black Arts Movement. He stands as a living reminder of one of the goals of many Movement artists—to use art in an effort to promote cultural and political education in the Black community, thereby encouraging the creation and support of the very institutions that fundamentally shape lives.

To understand Madhubuti's work, one must first turn to the Black Arts Movement, which dates from approximately 1965 to 1975. One of the most important movements in African-American literary history, this dynamic period of cultural enlightenment was fostered by artists and activists around the country. The most notable contributors were Amiri Baraka (LeRoi Jones), Sonia Sanchez, Ron Karenga, Larry Neal, Gwendolyn Brooks, Askia Toure, Ron Milner, and Ed Bullins. Along with Madhubuti, they shared common goals, which included the liberation, unification and empowerment of the Black community.

The Black Arts Movement is considered by many participants to be the artistic arm of the Black Power Movement. Both were extensions of the Civil Rights Movement. The Civil Rights Movement was an organized effort that culminated in the 1950s to abolish legislated segregation and extend democracy to all U.S. citizens, regardless of color. It was concerned with the separate and unequal treatment of African Americans who were supposedly citizens of a democratic society, but were denied many of the benefits and rights of such a society. As a freed people who had suffered the indignity of slavery for over 400 years in the Americas, Blacks were denied political rights, were legally forced to accept segregation, and were considered second-class citizens. They were also denied access to adequate public education. Indeed, Black Americans were a subordinate class forced to adhere to strict segregationist laws and customs as well as a caste system that prohibited them from attaining political, economic or social power.

Contrary to popular belief, Black resistance did not begin with the Civil Rights Movement of the 1950s. It was part of a history of Black resistance dating back to the Slave Era. This period, spanning from approximately 1619 to 1865, was marked by individual and collective rebellions on the part of enslaved Africans in North America in response to their lack of civil rights. Unable to own land, vote, read or write, these enslaved Africans were considered property of the slave owners who bought them, rendering them politically and socially powerless. Nevertheless, they resisted the circumstances and their oppressors. Through organized rebellions, slave narratives, and escape to states that outlawed slavery, music, dance, and other forms of resistance, a legacy of struggle was embedded in the history of enslaved Africans in North America.

That tradition of resistance continued to thrive through various philosophies of Black Nationalism, some of which later became infused into the Black Power Movement agenda. Eventually, a Black Nationalism voice emerged, personified by Malcolm X (formerly Malcolm Little). An ex-street hustler and convict, Malcolm X came to national attention through his articulation of the philosophy of the Nation of Islam, which was at that time headed by the Honorable Elijah Muhammad. Madhubuti, then Don L. Lee, was heavily influenced by Malcolm

X's activism in the Black community. That influence would later appear in his critical essays on politics and culture.

Along with Martin Luther King, Jr., Black Americans now had another leader, one who strongly and unapologetically pointed the finger at the contradictions between American idealism and practice. Malcolm X denounced the inhumane treatment Blacks suffered as impoverished, undereducated and exploited second-class citizens. His articulation of their frustration, along with his call for self-determination, led to a renewed sense of Black pride and cultural nationalism that would become the foundation of the Black Arts Movement.

Though many events and ideologies merged to form the Black Arts Movement, the most important contributing factors that led to its emergence included the surge of the Civil Rights Movement against Jim Crow and American hypocrisy regarding democracy, the rising voice of Malcolm X and others who demanded that Blacks assert themselves within a nationalist identity, the eventual murder of both Martin Luther King, Jr. and Malcolm X; the subsequent attempt to repress the Civil Rights Movement by the government, and the progression of the Black Power Movement from a demand for civil rights to a demand for power. Young leaders who preceded Madhubuti in this fight for power included Amiri Baraka (LeRoi Jones), Huey Newton, Robert F. Williams and Stokely Carmichael (Kwame Ture).

Thus, an artistic movement was fueled by the mass movement for civil rights, yet shaped by the demand for affirmation of an African American identity. In short, the Black Arts Movement grew out of the Civil Rights and the Black Power Movements, partly as a response to Malcolm X's call for self-determination, self-respect, self-reliance, and self-defense. Madhubuti would be at the forefront of this movement.

During the 1960s, young Black men and women were finding their voice as activists and intellectuals, all the while maturing in front of a world audience. They would influence others throughout the Diaspora to demand similar changes. Many espoused the belief that only real, measurable political, social and economic power would benefit the Black community. Their Black Nationalist stance manifested into the "Black Power" slogan used by countless organizations that sprang up in the midst of the 1960s and 1970s. The attraction to Black power to the young generation was very evident. The concept was mesmerizing, and Madhubuti was among those who were inspired to bravely stand up in the name of cultural pride and empowerment.

Black power politics was primarily concerned with government control over education and economic development. Activists like Madhubuti insisted that Blacks would have to take control of their own communities while some called on the government for more funding for community-based programs and improvement of education. Others focused on integrating the existing government with Black politicians who would speak and act on behalf of the Black community. Still others insisted that Blacks remain autonomous, creating their own economic and social institutions.

Amiri Baraka and other artists/activists heralded a call to arms—a call to artists to take action, not merely theorize. It was a passionate cry for work and dedication that attracted many Black artists. They began to see themselves and their work as agents of change. Madhubuti responded through participation in political organizations and through his writing, publishing poetry and essays that questioned Black middle class values while promoting Black power and unity.

A merger of working-class artists, political activists, and intellectuals took place on a national scale between 1967 and 1974 in cities such as Chicago, New York, San Francisco, Los Angeles, Milwaukee, Detroit, St. Louis and Philadelphia. Many looked inward to their own heritage, culture and traditions. They demanded a new, non-European aesthetic through which they could create and evaluate their art. Hoyt Fuller best summarized the black aesthetic, in his essay "Towards a Black Aesthetic" stating, "The young writers of the black ghetto have set out in search of a Black Aesthetic, a system of isolating and evaluating the artistic works of black people which reflect the special character and imperatives of Black experience." Madhubuti was greatly influenced by Fuller and others on this issue. In 1973, he wrote a collection of essays titled *From Plan to Planet: Life-Studies: The Need for Afrikan Minds and Institutions*. He alludes to the black aesthetic when he writes, "People define themselves in accordance with their own values using tradition and reason that is uniquely theirs."

As the Black Power Movement gained momentum, and the concept of Black power became familiar to millions of Americans, both Black and White, so too did the concept of the Black aesthetic gain popularity amongst Black artists nationwide. Thus, for many artists the Black aesthetic proved indispensable as they were engaged in creative activity led by a Black Nationalist agenda. Amiri Baraka encouraged Madhubuti and other Black writers to work from a cultural objective, one rooted in their own culture, instead of the dominant culture. Such work was essential to developing a consciousness that would eventually lead Madhubuti toward writing and activism that reflected a more complex understanding of cultural identity and aesthetics than he held prior to 1965.

In short, the Black Arts Movement provided a means of expression for cultural nationalists like Madhubuti who were committed to the empowerment of Black Americans through the use of art as a vital component of political activism. Madhubuti and his contemporaries forged new ideologies, reshaped old political theories, and expanded the Western concepts concerning art.

Whether one agrees with the political and theoretical changes Black Arts Movement artists supported, it is clear that this period in American literary history played a major part in changing American culture, specifically regarding Black self-awareness. Furthermore, it marked the beginning of a grassroots effort to undermine the domination of Western aesthetics in art produced by non-whites. For Madhubuti, the Black Arts Movement's effect on his work would prove extremely influential, especially given his simultaneous involvement in political organizations.

Despite his commitment to the tenets of the Black Arts Movement, critical reception of Madhubuti's early work was mixed. In 1971, Jeanne-Marie A. Miller noted his lack of originality in his collection of essays, *We Walk the Way of the New World*. Yet Miller also praised Madhubuti (then Don L. Lee), stating that he is "in the vanguard of revolutionary and avant-garde poets in this land." She concluded, however, that "the direction his poetry will travel in the distant future is unpredictable at this point."

Many reviewers shared Miller's positive assessment of Madhubuti's promise. In 1971, R. Roderick Palmer questioned Madhubuti's purpose: "What is Don L. Lee's hang-up? The answer seems to be concerned with his impatience with 'niggers' and 'Negroes' (he uses the terms synonymously) who refuse to be black, and with the 'little niggers killing little niggers.'" Palmer labeled Madhubuti's and other revolutionary poets' poetry as protest literature and asserted that his work stands as proof that "literature dealing with such serious subject matter, cannot, in essence, be simplistic, immature and unimportant," as suggested by Addison Gayle in his preface to *Black Expression*.

Earlier in Madhubuti's career, critics found his work racist and unworthy of praise. Jascha Kessler believed *Directionscore* (1971) to be propaganda. He criticized the poetry by questioning Madhubuti's sense of poetic language, emphatically stating that it could not be found in the work itself. Kessler further described Madhubuti's poetry using language that negates any artistic merit the work may have encompassed: "Anger, bombast, raw hatred, strident, aggrieved, perhaps charismatically crude religious and political canting, propaganda and racist nonsense, yes; and utterly unoriginal in form and style; humorless; cruel laughter bordering on the insane." Kessler continued, "What he has is street language, common enough to most of us; the rest is …rancid LeRoi Jones, mixed with editorials out of *Muhammad Speaks*."

Indeed, Kessler was not alone, for many critics of the Black Arts Movement found the use of Black English and non-traditional (or non-Western) poetic forms contrary to the very nature of poetry. However, this strategy was reflective of the Movement's agenda for many artists—to reach Black people through an affirmation of their culture. They argued that language is an important component of any culture; therefore, emphasizing cultural pride required respect and validation of the language used in the Black community. Like Madhubuti, they chose to dispel the myth that Black English was "bad English" through infusing it into their work.

Eugene Miller found Madhubuti's work unpoetic. In 1973, he questioned the accessibility of Madhubuti's work to non-black audiences. Madhubuti, according to Miller, searches for the "metaphors, the similes, the various figures of speech and allusions that poems are traditionally filled with and that necessitate a person (teacher) trained in literary analysis to use in interpreting poetry." Miller found himself excluded from Madhubuti's readership. Madhubuti's lack of concern for traditional Western poetic form alienated critics like Miller, thus marginalizing Madhubuti's success in mainstream publishing. Despite these early critics' opinions of Madhubuti's poetry, his work continued to evolve and take on more complex issues.

Madhubuti's poetry and essays produced during and since the Black Arts Movement are examined in chapters 2 and 3 to establish a clear understanding of his evolution as an artist and activist. These chapters also reveal how the two roles intersect in his work. Specifically, I wanted to discuss the major changes in his perspective and work, since it is clear that Madhubuti's work goes from a reactionary voice (found in the early poetry) to a more reflective and politically astute voice in his essays.

This book concludes with the transcript of an interview I conducted with Madhubuti in his office at Third World Press in Chicago. A large segment of the transcription is included so as to give readers Madhubuti's assessment of his life and art at present. It was most interesting to learn how Madhubuti feels about his choices, particularly the motivation behind them and how they have affected his family and politics. Readers will notice, for example, that he refers to the first person plural when speaking of major contributions. He does so, I believe, because he has a collective consciousness and is forever striving to work as part of the larger Black community. This is worth mentioning because so much of what makes him fascinating are the sacrifices he has made as an individual for the good of the collective black community.

The interview is also a major component of the book because I offer it to future researchers who find Madhubuti's work and life as important as I do. In fact, it is my greatest hope that the interview will inspire future scholars to expand the scholarship on Madhubuti and the Black Arts Movement since so much of what we see today in the work of spoken word artists is reminiscent of the Black Arts Movement beginnings, though there are obvious differences in the artists' political views.

As a man concerned with the well-being of his people, Haki Madhubuti remains a revolutionary. One finds such spirit in his art and in his immeasurable achievements. Ever concerned with the welfare of Black people, he stands as a symbol of Black power and unity for artists of his generation and generations to come. I certainly hope this book gives his readers and his toughest critics a closer look at the man and his legacy.

CHAPTER ONE

The
Pioneer
and
Positive
Prophet

The Pioneer and Positive Prophet

Haki R. Madhubuti was born Don L. Lee in Little Rock, Arkansas, on February 23, 1942. Though he isn't sure if his parents ever married, he is very clear on the details that shaped his life and worldview as a child. His mother Helen Maxine Graves Lee raised him alone, taking Madhubuti and his sister, Jacklyn, to Detroit where he stayed until 1959.

A victim of illiteracy and underemployment, his mother found it difficult to provide many necessities for her children. Eventually the family moved in with a man who became a surrogate stepfather for the children. This stepfather, however, did not serve as a positive role model. Though he worked to provide for his family, he was an alcoholic whose addiction led to domestic violence. His mother, also addicted to alcohol, tried to keep the family intact. In his 1978 introduction to *Enemies: The Clash of Races* Madhubuti wrote, "Every Monday morning I was sent to 'friends' to borrow money to get us through the week. I often had to walk five or ten miles to get this money...There was never any talk of education or of the future in our family." Madhubuti dreamed of becoming a trumpet player, but his dream was thwarted by the social and economic disparity he and his family faced.

Such early childhood experiences would have lasting effects on his life as an activist during the 1960s and 1970s. Because of his early introduction to economic and social disparity, he turned toward serious writing and political struggle as a young adult. Madhubuti's understanding of the oppression urban Blacks suffered due to unemployment, as well as his eyewitness experience with drug and alcohol abuse, would later contribute to his complex political ideologies. In *Ground-Work* (1996), he maintains, "My environment is critical to my understanding of the world and my (our) place in it. Growing up poor automatically positioned me with the overwhelming majority of the world's people and I didn't need Marx to tell me to fight oppression, whether economic or political." Later he would write about this early experience, specifically his mother's death—when he was sixteen—stating that it forced manhood upon him, but stimulated him enough to begin to question the world around him.

As a teenager, Madhubuti took several odd jobs to support himself, including cleaning taverns after hours and delivering newspapers. After moving to Chicago to live with an aunt, he worked at a broom factory and collected junk to sell. However, it was his determination that motivated him to stay in school. Consequently, he graduated from Chicago's Dunbar High School in 1960. These early adolescent experiences, along with the harsh realities of racism, would be the building blocks to his activism in his early twenties. Knowing the frustrations felt by most Blacks in urban America, Madhubuti would rely on his experiences to shape a political agenda for the Black community.

In addition to his personal experiences with racism, Madhubuti also found fault with the Black community. In particular, he believed the Black church to be hypocritical and alienating. As a child in Detroit, he questioned the motives of those who went to the church next door to his mother's home—those who refused to actually live in the neighborhood because of its low-income residents. In fact, the class differences within the Black community also became painfully clear to him as a child. Once, dressed in a secondhand sport coat, he ventured into the neighborhood church, only to be teased by the other children there. "I just wanted to meet those other people in there. So I put on my little used sport coat and used pants and it was just very painful the way the kids treated me. I was introduced to a level of cruelty among upper-class Black children that I've never forgotten."

As an adult he became more disillusioned with the Black church. Although it was a Black institution, he found it lacking in its service to the community. Instead, he saw many churches catering to the needs of their middle-class congregations, ignoring the quality of life forced upon most Blacks. Such disappointment with the Black church fed an early desire on his part to reconstruct Black institutions, which he believed should foster unity, not division. Critical of Black institutions that only supported "Negro" attitudes and the Black middle class, a more politically astute Madhubuti would later declare war on such institutions during the 1970s.

At age thirteen, one profound experience impacted the rest of his life. He visited the local library to check out *Black Boy* by Richard Wright. He recalled this moment, "You must understand that at that time this whole question of identity was never a large part of my consciousness. In the Black community you still had white is right, yellow is mellow, brown stick around and Black step back. And so we were instilled in that kind of ethos, which was really tearing the community apart." This ethos was particularly profound to him, and he addressed the issue of "colorism" and self-hatred in later collections of essays and poems.

Despite the shame he felt in asking the librarian for books about Blacks, a sympathetic librarian aided Madhubuti in his various searches. However, when it came to *Black Boy*, he stated, "I was ashamed of being Black but she prevailed and I went and found the book on the shelf myself, because I didn't want to ask a White librarian for *Black Boy*." Reading the book was significant to him because the book mirrored so much of his own life. He explained, "It was just struggle all the time. It's like you're forced to be a man when you haven't hit boyhood yet." For Madhubuti, these childhood lessons eventually aided him in his development of the practical theories that he supported in the struggle for Black liberation. In addition, his interest in Pan-Africanism, cultural nationalism and revolutionary nationalism is evidence of these early lessons.

Much of Richard Wright's work also influenced Madhubuti in that he was introduced to Communism through one of Wright's essays. Thus, Wright became a teacher/role model for him, in absentia, for he was influenced by Wright's art, as well as his life experiences. He explained, "I've never been pulled into the [political] Left like a lot of our intellectuals because I understood clearly what Wright went through in terms of trying to be an artist."

An incident that took place after he'd joined the Army made him even more aware of the importance of literature and the potential power it can offer readers. After getting off the bus at boot camp, Madhubuti held in his hands a copy of Paul Robeson's memoirs. The white sergeant snatched the book away, claiming Robeson was a "Black Communist" and began to rip pages from the book in front of Madhubuti. At that crucial moment, he was certain that he would never again apologize for being Black; he would re-educate himself by reading everything available on or by Black people; he would begin to write himself; and since the ideas of Robeson frightened people like the sergeant so much, he would go into the "idea business." He stated, "I began to sharpen my mind to the point where it will be my major weapon. And that's what I've been doing all my life."

While in the Army, Madhubuti began to read a variety of books, many of which helped to shape the political theories he would later espouse. He read, on average, a book a day, specifically reading everything he could get his hands on about Black people. Of this time, he stated, "I had a very elementary understanding of what was happening. I understood then that we, being Black folks, are in a very disadvantaged position in this country. And that nothing was fair in terms of economics, politics and education. So I knew that whatever I ended up doing, or we ended up doing, was going to require an awful lot of work, a lot of struggle."

After filling up on the available literature of Black people, he decided that if he were going to contribute to any change in the Black community, he would have to write. As a result, he developed a ritual of writing a 250-word essay after every book he read while still in the Army, thus strengthening his writing and critical thinking skills. At this time he made another valuable decision that would reflect on his endeavors: he decided that only he, not the Army nor the dominant culture as a whole, would determine his destiny.

During his stint in the Army, Madhubuti was introduced to Margaret and Charlie Burroughs, Leftist activists and founders of Chicago's DuSable Museum. Since the Burroughs were dedicated to educating the public about Black art and Blacks' contributions to the world of art throughout the course of history, his attraction to them and the museum was natural. He volunteered at the museum for four years, from 1962 to 1966, learning from the Burroughs' various theories and histories on political activism and struggles throughout the world. Volunteering provided another important opportunity, for as an assistant curator, he was able to meet Russian delegates, study the works of Russian writers and engage in conversations about Leftist politics with the Burroughs and other scholars. Such tutelage would come to be extremely helpful when he became an active organizer, specifically when he later joined the Congress of African People, which suffered a split within the organization because of Leftist politics.

In 1966, he self-published his first book of poetry, *Think Black!* As the Black Power Movement began to gain momentum, Madhubuti sold copies of the book during rallies and other public events related to the Movement. Such work was essential to new writers like Madhubuti because of his earlier decision to avoid large publishing houses altogether. To him, the act of selling books of poetry to people who would not ordinarily read poetry was revolutionary in and of itself. "I'd stand at 63rd and Cottage Grove under the elevated [subway train] and sell the books." Eventually Madhubuti attended Wilson Junior College (now Kennedy King Community College) and began working with the Congress of Racial Equality (CORE).

At that time, he also began to write poetry regularly and this brought him into contact with the idea of publishing more work and also introduced him to two noted Black publishers. Dudley Randall, the publisher of Broadside Press, showed an interest in his early poetry, specifically after he'd published *Think Black!* In addition, Hoyt Fuller, managing editor of *Negro Digest*, also found his work dynamic and worthy of publication. Both Randall and Fuller would later forge a close relationship with Madhubuti in their shared commitment to publishing Black literature and building Black institutions.

By 1967, Madhubuti had captured the attention of the activists involved in the Black liberation struggle. His poems then voiced their anger and demands and symbolized the growing interest in African-centered values and aesthetics. Madhubuti began working with Chicago's Organization of Black American Culture (OBAC) and its writers' workshop, then under the guidance of Fuller.

That summer he met Gwendolyn Brooks at a writing workshop on Chicago's South Side. They would later become each other's biggest fan. In fact, Brooks eventually left Harper & Row Publishers for Randall's Broadside Press and eventually Madhubuti's Third World Press, marking a turning point in her career. In recalling this important artistic relationship, Madhubuti believes "her example and her support, her cultural and emotional support, and her financial support have been the key in terms of [my] development."

However, such sentiment contrasts Madhubuti's early criticism of Brooks' work. In 1970, his harsh statements about her celebrated *Annie Allen* are found in the preface of Brooks' first autobiography *Report From Part One* (1970). In it, he stated that the work was written for White readers instead of Black readers, and insisted that the book was concerned with poetics. Brooks, too, criticized his work, calling the use of profanity by younger Black Arts Movement writers unnecessary. After walking away from a heated discussion with Brooks, Madhubuti met with her to discuss their different perspectives on language. Eventually, they were able to move past their differences and build a committed friendship that spanned several decades.

In fact, their relationship became one of friendship marked by strong artistic collaboration. One sees the influence he had on her work after 1967, when Brooks proclaimed a cultural awakening and shift in voice that redirected her work toward Black readers and culture. She also developed an appreciation for his work when she called him her "spiritual son." At Chicago State University, where he currently teaches, Madhubuti founded the Gwendolyn Brooks Center for Creative Writing and Black Literature, which encourages and educates young writers and hosts an annual writer's conference. Madhubuti continues to speak of Brooks with great admiration, calling her legacy a national treasure.

Her death in 2000 was a difficult loss for Madhubuti as well as those she influenced through her work and efforts. In examining her influences on his life and others' lives, Madhubuti said of Brooks, "She would rank at the top of the list in terms of influences and in terms of examples, probably as a writer-activist. Her activism is more in terms of dealing with young people and children and not necessarily on a national or local scene in terms of leading anybody. Her activism is in sharing her work and trying to encourage young people to express themselves in poetry."

In 1967 Madhubuti published his second book of poetry, *Black Pride*, which was published by Broadside Press with an introduction by its president and, by then, personal friend, Dudley Randall. This collection was well received by both writers and activists. His political activism by this time also increased as he began working with civil rights organizations such as the CORE. As many have previously noted, political activism characterized the 1960s as the government labeled many Black Nationalists dangerous threats to national security. Madhubuti's involvement, however, increased. He stated of this time, "Around '67-68, J. Edgar Hoover, under his leadership, the FBI initiated COINTELPRO, which was a counter-intelligence program to disrupt the Black movement. He had targeted mainly the major Civil Rights organizations: SCLC (the Southern Christian Leadership Conference), NAACP (the National Association for the Advancement of Colored People) and CORE. He did not know too much about the underground movement until the Black Panthers hit and they were targeted, as well as other groups."

Madhubuti's response to such political activity was to simply publish his poetry. As an emerging Black poet, he would put forth his energies toward support of Black liberation by reaching the Black masses through his art. In 1968, Madhubuti published *For Black People (and Negroes Too)*, a four-page broadside. Also at this time he started speaking at colleges and universities around the country. By age twenty-seven he was invited to teach at both Cornell University (despite some resistance from the search committee, due to his lack of academic credentials) and Talledega College in Alabama. He accepted the offer at Cornell and, after a year at Cornell, published another poetry collection, *Don't Cry, Scream* (1969), with an introduction by Gwendolyn Brooks, which sold over 250,000 copies.

This catapulted him to national celebrity and he became one of the few Black writers to become a household name.

In March of that same year, *Ebony Magazine* published an article about him, catapulting him further into national celebrity status. The article, written by David Llorens, highlights his position as writer–in–residence at Cornell University. Llorens includes Madhubuti's initial reaction to Cornell's offer, stating, "At first he refused, preferring instead to occupy a similar position at a Black college in Alabama. It was all but settled when the sun gave way to cloudburst—the Black college wasn't ready for Don Lee.... The paradox—that he was accepted at a white college for the same qualities that caused rejection at a Black college—makes Don laugh with disgust."

One can look at the *Ebony Magazine* article as a major contribution to Madhubuti's popularity in the Black community. Despite the poet's insistence of writing for and about Black people, both as critic and observer, Madhubuti was still unknown to many working-class and middle-class Blacks who did not identify with the Black Arts Movement or the Black Power Movement. The article brought Madhubuti to them, introducing him as an innovator, activist and genius poet who is "a lion of a poet who splits syllables, invents phrases, makes letters work as words, and gives rhythmic quality to verse that is never savage but often vicious and always reflecting a revolutionary Black consciousness."

Interestingly, Madhubuti's political activism increased as he became more famous as a writer. After Cornell, he eventually accepted a position at Howard University, commuting weekly from Chicago to Washington, D.C. for eight years. In addition to his difficult work schedule, he also founded Third World Press in 1967 and the Institute for Positive Education/New Concept School in 1969. Both were manifestations of a personal belief—that intellectuals must be directly involved in the struggle for Black unity and power. He stated of these two endeavors, "I'd always felt the publishing company is important, but I've got this activist spirit so I have one spirit saying, 'okay, the books' and another spirit saying, 'we have to deal with these children,' and [so] we started the Institute of Positive Education."

Two common themes that run through his early poems from the 1960s and 1970s and his essays written from the late 1970s to the present are unity and power in the Black community. These themes are part of his cultural, nationalist beliefs, which symbolize a strong commitment to struggle, institution building and African-centered values. One finds these themes in his earliest poems from *Think Black!* (1966) through his work in *Run Toward Fear* (2004).

As a leading figure in the Black Arts Movement, Madhubuti is important because he not only influenced his peers—artists and activists alike—but also posed significant questions about the fate of Black Americans and the role Black Nationalism would play in the future of the country. His agenda was twofold: to challenge Black Americans to accept an African-centered worldview from which to fight social, economic and political oppression, and to create a pro-Black aesthetic in art. He quickly gained popularity during the Black Arts Movement for his unyielding beliefs and bold voice, which demanded the attention of both white and Black America. His brashness and bravery were essential to a movement that is considered by some scholars to be one of the most innovative literary movements in African American history.

But the Movement, despite its profound influence on Black literature and its reception around the world, was not without its faults. There were concerns, for example, about the role of the Black artist, as defined by the leaders of the Movement. Many of the artists were led by a sincere desire to use art as a political response to Western racist aesthetics, while others felt that defining one's art by the color of one's skin was limiting and damaging to any work's overall effect. Madhubuti and others were ultimately concerned with the function of art. How would it best serve Blacks in their struggle for freedom from racism and oppression? How could the art teach and guide the masses toward a more African–centered value system and lifestyle?

Madhubuti's stand on such questions can be found in his poetry from that time. Because of the evolution he undergoes as a political activist, his growth as an artist is often reflected in his poetry. Marlene Mosher's theory, which links Madhubuti's development as an activist/writer to that of Frantz Fanon's theory pertaining to revolutionary development (detailed in Fanon's *Wretched of the Earth*, 1963), provides some understanding of Madhubuti's evolution as a writer. Fanon's discourse was a source of theoretical inspiration for many political activists during the Black Arts Movement. In fact, Madhubuti often quoted Fanon in his earlier essays, as did many of his contemporaries.

Today, Haki Madhubuti is still an active member of organizations aimed at empowering Black people throughout the Diaspora. He has stated, "Ideas, creative ideas, run the world. And that has always been my point.... It's one thing to sit down and have the ideas, but it becomes another thing to take the idea from the written page and implement it. That is what this has been about, implementation." He holds strong to an unyielding belief that the goal of Black power and unity cannot be realized without great effort on the part of all Blacks to define themselves as independent of Western values and aesthetics. *In Enemies: The Clash of Races*, he states,

> Under the banner of being 'human' or 'spiritual' or 'ideologically correct' we meet, socialize and make 'love' with our enemies ...we blindly give our allegiance to governments, ideologies, religions or corporations that day to day meet our most elementary or physical needs, but these same governments, ideologies, religions and corporations (who are all white) have never worked in the best interest of Black people. We push anti-Black concepts and values such as western individualism and capitalist or communist materialism and would break into a fever at the mention of anything Black.

In general, Madhubuti's poetry and essays have been hailed as "revolutionary," but remarkably remain ignored within mainstream academic scholarship. Criticism on his work is insufficient as many literary scholars see him as a political activist only, while activists perceive him, first and foremost, as a writer. Moreover, his insistence on working only with small, independent Black presses has undoubtedly limited the size of his readership. He remains focused, however, and ever–willing to accept the consequences of his decisions. He has stated, "I think that we all limit ourselves and our own capabilities. I don't care about your credentials in the final analysis. I think in the final analysis, what will define all of us is what one has contributed."

Indeed, Madhubuti has made few concessions in his life and work. He has maintained that one's "outsider" status is often a safer, more advantageous space to occupy. For him, it is a place of comfort, one in which his autonomy is not frequently tested or challenged by mainstream capitalist values. Thus, he has occupied this space throughout his entire career, as both an artist and an entrepreneur. By refusing to allow large mainstream publishing houses to publish his work, he proudly insists, "Out of the writers and poets who have emerged out of the sixties and essentially made a major contribution, I'm the only one who has not been published by White publishers. [Not at all, or only when Blacks do anthologies.] In terms of books, one hundred percent of my books have been published by Black publishers."

Madhubuti also believes that education is an essential part of empowering any community. His commitment to Black liberation is evident in his establishment (along with his wife, Safisha Madhubuti) of the Institute of Positive Education/New Concept School and the Betty Shabazz International Charter School, two independent schools in Chicago. The innovative teaching strategies used at these schools have become so popular that the schools' administrators and faculty offer teacher-training seminars for educators from other schools who are interested in developing curriculum specifically for Black students. Located on Chicago's Southside and in a predominately Black neighborhood, the schools serve as an alternative to parents who demand more for their children than traditional public and private schools provide.

For Madhubuti, one's politics are an integral part of one's identity. His own personal involvement in political organizations is evident in his memberships and in his leadership roles dating back to the 1960s, when he was involved in the Black Power Movement and several progressive political organizations, including the CORE, the Student Non-violent Coordinating Committee (SNCC) and SCLC. In addition, he is a former executive council member of the Congress of African People, and he served on the executive council for the historic Million Man March. Along with his participation in organized political activities, Madhubuti has traveled extensively as an advocate for political change. He has made frequent trips to Africa as a member of the African Liberation Support Committee and has been asked to speak all over the world, including Asia and Africa.

The Black Arts Movement artists were motivated by the belief that one must always rely on one's culture and community as sources of strength and power. For Madhubuti, this is problematic if both are detrimental to the people and if Blacks' understanding of culture and community has been tainted by a delusional value system espoused through Western culture. As both pioneer and positive prophet, he has maintained for over forty years a clear, steady commitment toward restoring and empowering Black people and Black life.

The
Poetry of
Empowerment

CHAPTER TWO
The Poetry of Empowerment

THE BLACK ARTS MOVEMENT

Haki Madhubuti's debut as a published poet came when he penned and self-published his first work in 1966, a collection of poetry titled *Think Black!* Poetry became his weapon of choice in a politically charged society that demanded silence from marginalized groups like African Americans. In the late 1960s, he and other Black artists, such as Amiri Baraka (LeRoi Jones), Larry Neal, Sonia Sanchez, and Mari Evans, insisted on promoting an aesthetic in their own image and the interest of Blacks. They wrote in the tradition of Black activists before them, who saw the connection between art and activism as a necessary one for liberation, and they insisted that their work respond to the issues of the time. Indeed, they would use their work to fight against the ideologies and power structures that oppressed Black people worldwide.

In addition, Madhubuti used (and continues to use) his art to develop practical solutions to political, social and economic oppression Blacks face. Like many cultural nationalists, he saw his role as cultural artist as an active one that demanded personal maturation and sincere commitment to the struggle for Black liberation. Thus, he could not simply be an artist divorced from the political struggle in which Blacks were engaged. Instead, he believed that his position as artist—one who records the images, hopes and reality of the masses—demanded he commit himself to political action, not merely rhetoric.

One can see in Madhubuti's development as a Black Nationalist and writer a long, reflective journey. His work reveals the painful process of first recognizing his own anger, then presenting solutions to the problems which plague Black America. Perhaps that is what separates him from many other cultural activists/artists. The primary elements inherent in his work are a sense of eternal optimism and practical application. In short, his poetry challenges Blacks to realistically examine their condition and then act to change it.

Moreover, Madhubuti articulates solutions through the use of a revolutionary poetic voice, a voice that channels messages through poetry, demanding change in attitude, change in self-perception and change in actions. Over time this voice naturally progresses, like the artist himself, and becomes more astute and self-assured; it becomes a voice that directs and challenges its readers. In his poetry, this voice is both critical and comforting, often simultaneously reflecting a leader/member persona of the Black community. Similarly, it is through development of this poetic voice that Madhubuti has remained loyal to the concept of the artist as a political change agent, using his art to incite Black unity and power. In fact, as Madhubuti's personal politics become clearer, so does his poetry.

For Madhubuti, writing was not a goal, as it did not appear to lead one toward financial success. Once he entered military service, however, and began to see the fear Whites had of Black revolutionary literature, he understood the effective power of language. He understood that Black literature that was affirming and encouraged in readers a desire for cultural liberation was indeed feared and that literature could be used as a weapon of resistance against cultural superiority. The early collections, (*Think Black!*, *Black Pride*, *For Black People*, *Don't Cry, Scream*, *We Walk the Way of the New World*, *Directionscore* and *Book of Life*), which date from 1966 to 1973, show Madhubuti acting as both spokesperson for and critic of the Black community, chastising those who wear their Blackness like a trend and praising those who celebrate their culture through words and political activity. In these poems one hears his call for Blacks to build institutions in and for their communities to empower themselves overall, and to reject corrupt Western values and capitalism. Throughout all of his early poetry, however, is a distinct celebration of culture, where the speakers in these poems articulate a strong Black Nationalist stance while seeking a dialogue with readers.

Following Maulana Karenga's Kawaida, a cultural value system based on seven principles, Madhubuti would express urgency for change in Blacks' attitudes, actions, and loyalty to a Black nation. Black art should reflect the people who create it and are subjects of it. Thus, Madhubuti's poetry acts as an outgrowth of such criteria in that its dual purpose appears to be concerned with Black power, Black unity and the investigation of new ideas. Madhubuti says he and Karenga "began to work together around projects and tried to move in the same direction as Pan-African Nationalists." He further said of his relationship with Karenga, "[He] is one of the most brilliant men that I know. He has a superior mind. *Introduction to Black Studies* is one of the seminal works out there."

Think Black! was the first of many books of poetry and essays by Madhubuti that examine the dilemmas of race relations, Black power and Black unity in America and the Diaspora. Grounded in a strong desire to express his rage toward the dominant culture's use of race as a means of oppression, Madhubuti, then Don L. Lee, began to write poems intended to cause Blacks to actually change their "slave mentality" or colonial thinking—to think through a new concept of self that allows race to act as a positive descriptor.

THE POEMS

Madhubuti was very focused on his intended response: to incite Black readers to act. He wanted them to change—and change not only their own individual lives but also the community of Blacks as a whole.

In short, he wanted to increase Black power through his art. The book's title is evidence of Madhubuti's purpose: he is calling for Black power and action while insisting that before such action can occur, there must be a change in self–perception and values. Blacks, in other words, must change their definition of Blackness. For Madhubuti, Blackness is equated with positive images, often African images, and stands opposite to the negative connotations White America has assigned it. Thus, Blackness is to be revered, celebrated and embraced, not altered, degraded or shunned.

In *Think Black!* Madhubuti challenges a mentally colonized people to see beauty in their culture rather than negate it. As a result, *Think Black!* (self-published by Madhubuti and later published by Broadside Press) marks the beginning of Madhubuti's call for psychological change in the Black man, woman and child. He reflects on the time in his life when he benefited from having lighter colored skin than some Blacks: "I, / at one time / loved / my / color " (1-5) because it "opened sMall / doors of tokenism" (6-9). He further writes:

> i
> began
> to love
> only a
> part of
> me—
> my inner
> self which
> is all
> black—
> &
> developed a
> vehement
> hatred of
> my light
> brown
> outer.

He denounces the compromises he endured prior to becoming enlightened about the importance of Black unity. His confession is wrought with the guilt he felt for having taken advantage of color discrimination, of having benefited from something that explicitly separates him from other blacks and demeans his culture.

Many artists/activists involved in the Black Arts Movement wanted to encourage a sense of pride in the Black community, to invent images and symbols that would promote a healthy Black pride in every Black man, woman and child. This is directly related to the agenda of the Black cultural nationalists who believed that culture is organic to people. It is, thus, easy to assume that during the early stages of his career, Madhubuti wanted to use his poetry to add positive symbols and images to Black culture to strengthen the Black nation.

However, in *Think Black!* he offers few positive images. Instead, he simply recognizes the practices and concepts that defeat Black America mentally and politically. As a result, this collection falls short in promoting a true revolutionary voice, for it could not be counted on to provide the solutions needed to solve the problems Blacks then faced. According to Mosher, *Think Black!* is more "a volume of 'reaction' than a volume of 'action'; as such it concerns itself more with the destruction of established White values than it does with the construction of new Black values."

Yet there is the beginning of a revolutionary voice in *Think Black!* that offers solutions, though not as fine-tuned as in subsequent volumes. In *Think Black!* Madhubuti insists that Blacks reorient themselves and accept their own culture instead of White mainstream culture. Thus, he emerges, according to some critics, as a cultural stabilizer whose mission is to reintroduce values from which Blacks can develop independent of destructive European values.

It is in Madhubuti's second volume of poetry, *Black Pride* (1967), that one hears a clearer revolutionary voice that promotes Black unity and pride. In *Black Pride* he spends less time lashing out at racism and chooses to focus on the Black middle class. In "The New Integrationist," he writes:

```
i
seek
integration
of
negroes
with
black
people.
```
(1-8)

The poem strongly suggests not only a difference in being black and being Negro, but also the hope on the speaker's part to unite the two factions within the Black community. It is a reflection of Madhubuti's understanding of the clash of race and class within the Black community.

As a developing Black Nationalist whose work in political organizations brings him toward a more complex understanding of politics and race dynamics, Madhubuti reflects his disdain of those Blacks who seek the approval of Whites. *Black Pride* also voices his concerns about the lack of power—economic, political and social—in the Black community. Such concern is a hallmark in his evolution as a writer and activist. Most of the poems in *Black Pride* are concerned with recognizing the problems Blacks face in White America—understanding capitalism, the differences between European and African aesthetics and values, etc.

Yet the poems in *Black Pride* do not yet provide an example of Madhubuti's later true revolutionary voice, which is one concerned with solutions. This does not mean that Madhubuti's work has not evolved. On the contrary, the revolutionary voice in these poems is more solid and less reactionary. He is clearly more confident in his writing style in *Black Pride*. One senses a mature cultural critic emerging in poems like "The Primitive":

```
taken from the
shores of Mother Africa.
the savages they thought
we were—
```

they being the real savages.
……………………………
Christianized us.
roped our minds with:
t.v. & straight hair,
reader's digest & bleaching creams,

…………………………..
Those alien concepts
of whi-teness,
the being of what
is not

(1-5, 10-13, 18-21)

This poem speaks of the horrors of slavery, not in terms of the physical abuse Blacks suffered, but the psychological war that was waged. Madhubuti focuses on cultural nationalism, strengthening the Black community by rejecting Western values and the demeaning images of Blackness. He is in line with Karenga's definition of Black Nationalism: "The revolution being fought now is a revolution to win the minds of our people."

Though the first two volumes are concerned with the same subject matter—power—*Don't Cry, Scream* (1969) is more concrete in providing positive Black images and plans for action. In this volume, he does not simply describe the problems Blacks face in America; rather, his revolutionary voice seeks to move his readers toward collective action. In addition, the title suggests the thrust of the volume—that action, not slogans or rhetoric, is needed. Like other Black cultural nationalists, Madhubuti promoted a Black value system by incorporating the ideas of Black unity and power into his art. Both Amiri Baraka and Madhubuti espoused a belief that Black artists should promote African-based values in their art. If they chose to do otherwise, the art would reflect an acceptance of the European Western aesthetic that they believed has been detrimental to the Blacks.

With *Don't Cry, Scream* it is obvious that Madhubuti is in line with the tenets of the Black Arts Movement, specifically when illustrating the harm of such assimilation. This is a departure from the two previous volumes, especially in the descriptors used for those Blacks who align themselves with White culture. For instance, while the "Negro" was a threat to Black unity in *Black Pride*, she or he is equated with a lowly animal in *Don't Cry, Scream*.

In the poem "Hero," Madhubuti articulates the hypocrisy of assimilation:

> little willie
> a hero in
> the american tradition.
> a blk/hero.
>
> (4.1-4)

The subject of the poem, Willie, is a black veteran who dies for his country only to receive his medals posthumously. Madhubuti tells readers of the various medals Willie received (e.g. the Purple Heart, Good Conduct) to illustrate the point that Blacks, regardless of their accomplishments and acceptance of American values, are always at risk of being denied justice. Willie's death is symbolic of the obstacles and ostracism Blacks face daily in America, despite their sacrifices and willingness to contribute to the nation's freedom.

Madhubuti made his role as artist/activist very clear in *Don't Cry, Scream*. His revolutionary voice urges Blacks to change their ways and wake-up to the nation's hypocrisy. In doing so, he demonstrates the use of Black poetry, which he states should "negate the negative influences of the mass media."

He continues to evolve in voice and message in his fourth volume of poetry, *We Walk the Way of the New World* (1970). In this volume, he continued to promote more direct messages and solutions for the problems plaguing the Black community while moving into more sophisticated and complex messages and imagery.

The book is divided into three parts: Black woman poems, African poems and New World poems. "Each section," he writes in the introduction, "is part of the other: Blackwoman is African and Africa is Blackwoman and they both represent the New World." This illustrates a more focused revolutionary voice, one that still seeks change but is more succinct and assured than in earlier collections. This specific interest in strategically arranging the poems is again supported by the poet's claim that Western aesthetic and values have corrupted Black Americans. He insists that by accepting "the European frame of reference," Blacks' standards of beauty have been tainted, thus creating an anti-Black standard of beauty. As a result, Blacks have learned to hate themselves because of their African features—hair, complexion, lips, eyes, etc.

A poem that demonstrates this self-hatred is "Blackman/An Unfinished History." He attempts to explain the transformation Blacks went through upon becoming Americans, thus losing their African values:

> we acquired a new ethic a new morality a new
> history
> and we lost
> we lost much we lost that that was
> we became americans   the best the real
> and blindly adopted america's heroes as our own
> and minds wouldn't function.
>
> (1.17-22)

The poem asserts that in becoming Americanized, Blacks lost important parts of themselves, including self-respect and pride in their own heroes and culture. Consequently, it became commonplace for Blacks to imitate Whites' beauty rituals (thereby believing blonde hair and blue eyes were necessities in achieving beauty) and artistic aesthetics (e.g. European forms and theories for writers, musicians, dancers, etc.).
In "Soft, Hard, Warm, Sure" Madhubuti calls attention to the Black woman, depicting an image of her which contradicts the demeaning stereotypes often used to depict her; stereotypes that are often perpetuated by Blacks themselves.

> soft: the way her eyes view her children.
> hard: her hands; a comment on her will.
> warm: just the way she is, jim!
> sure: as yesterday, she's tomorrow's tomorrow.
>
> (1-4)

In this poem, Madhubuti portrays the many facets and strengths of the black woman—mother, worker, lover, and future of the race—simply and subtly. He lifts her from the historical degradation that has influenced the way Blacks and others perceive her.

Unlike his first three volumes of poetry, this fourth volume is more sure in form and content. In these poems, one finds a poet whose visions of a powerful and united Black nation are clearer and stronger because of the subtlety in the verse. He no longer needs to plead with White America or chastise the Black middle class. This volume is in many ways less aggressive than the first three volumes, yet emerges more powerful in content and tone. *We Walk the Way of the New World* is filled with an assurance that Blacks can look forward to a new world, one filled with African values, and one devoid of self–hatred and degradation. It is clear that he selects poems that show him as a mature poet, one who has passed through political and artistic phases to emerge a cultural stabilizer. This collection encapsulates his earlier growth and his later period of reflection, and illuminates where he stands at the end of his growth cycle. His fifth book, *Directionscore* (1971), offers further direction, and it also displays the poet's early poetry and the journey he has traveled.

Directionscore includes poems from the his four volumes of poetry along with five new poems. Mosher contends, "Because Lee's [Madhubuti's] intention in *Directionscore* was to provide positive direction, he carefully culled most of the negative poems that had appeared in his first two volumes." Perhaps this was an indication of Madhubuti's awareness of his evolving consciousness and talent.

This collection continues to follow the direction of the last volume as it applauds those who work toward a positive, new world for Blacks while criticizing those who negate their future. In "Positives: For Sterling Plumpp" he writes:

> didn't u know u were lost brother?
> confused hair with blackness
> thought u knew it before the knower did,
> didn't u know u lost brother?

(2.10-13)

The speaker chastises Blacks who attempt to wear their "blackness" through hairstyles and clothing. This is certainly not a new message in Madhubuti's work, yet his use of language fused with a seasoned political career challenges readers to not only comprehend the "Negro mentality" but reconcile it within themselves.

However, some critics such as Mosher found that Madhubuti failed to take a new stance in *Directionscore*. Poems such as "A Poem for Black Women" and "Malcolm Spoke/Who Listened" show little difference in theme from poems in earlier collections. Nevertheless, this collection marks a period of reflection.

By 1973, many of the groups so important to the Black Power Movement felt the sting of government crackdowns and the effects of rampant drug abuse. Though the Black Power Movement was still strong in its efforts to incite demands for improvements in the Black community, Black artists began to channel their energies toward less visible activities, such as teaching, scholarship, parenting and working as administrators of social programs they fought for in the late 1960s. It is important to note, however, that many, Madhubuti included, continued to produce art and remained politically active.

In Madhubuti's sixth volume, *Book of Life* (1973), he is still a proponent of African values (and rejection of destructive European ones). In the book's foreword he writes, "This work comes at a difficult time in our lives. Comes at a period when we, as a race, are under much weight and can smell and feel the call of death in our very midst." He continues to call for unity amongst Blacks, but this volume does more than merely speak of the need for unity; it demands it. The poetry is more than simple Black power rhetoric, already a mainstay in the works of other Black writers. Instead, these poems serve as a wake-up call for those who have become wayward in their work as revolutionaries. The poems remind the readers that only through consistent discipline and work toward Black unity can true nation building begin. He writes, "We have become our own worst enemy—a cliché, yes, but oh so true."

In *Book of Life* Madhubuti criticizes those Black artists who have become traitors. The revolutionary voice found in his earlier works is more cynical and resentful here. He had obviously grown tired of those who did not work toward Black power and unity. These poems seem to have come from frustration, as he appears ready to see a tangible response to his previous work and spiritual messages. The poems in *Book of Life* reflect his increasing advocacy of economic prosperity for Blacks via Black-owned businesses, revitalized Black communities, and an African-centered curriculum in schools in Black neighborhoods.

Though Madhubuti has worked consistently to promote these things in his own life, one senses his disappointment that others do not heed the call. In *Book of Life* not only is he frustrated with Black artists and Blacks in general, but he is also frustrated with white establishments that have denied Blacks the opportunities and rights they have fought for during the Black Power Movement. In "We Are Some Funny 'Black Artists'" he writes about the hypocrisy found in mainstream publishing houses that exploit Black revolutionary writers and their causes:

> random house and double day publish the
> "militant black writers"
> who write real-bad about the
> "money-hungry jew" and the "power-crazed
>   irishman"
> random house and double day will continue to
>   publish
> "militant black writers"
> ....
> while the
> "militant black writers"
> who write real-bad about white people
> can't even get a current accounting of their
> royalties from random house or double day
> and black nation-building never crossed their
> minds.
>
> (1-5, 12-17)

Madhubuti's frustration is also found in poems such as "Hooked," in which he writes of the growing drug problem that paralyzes the Black community and makes Black nation building almost impossible:

> the only time
> the brother is sober is
> when he tryin to
> find another
> high.
>
> (1-5)

He separates unreliable and reliable Black men in "Afrikan Men" by creating two groups: those who

> …have learned
> not to trust the easy music
> not to trust the processed food
> not to trust the comfortable compromise,
> have learned
> that love will not stop the enemies of the world
>
> (3.15-18)

Afrikan men, he contends, are smarter. They know that "if a rat is chewing at yr baby's skull/ you don't negotiate you/kill it" (3.22-25).

Perhaps the most practical poem in *Book of Life* is "Life Poems," a series of ninety-one quotable lessons, ranging from advice for living spiritually ("meditation is needed and necessary"), intellectually ("knowledge is like water/it is nourishment for those who seek it") and physically ("choose your food as you choose your friends"). This series of lessons echo Madhubuti's essays, as he moves away from the poetic voice toward a more spiritual-scholar voice.

Book of Life demonstrates Madhubuti's acceptance as a cultural stabilizer who continues to denounce anything that is destructive to Blacks and their future. Sometimes alone, sometimes with the collective assurance of others, he continues to use his poetic voice against the very systems that endanger Black life and culture. By the time the seventh volume of poetry, *Earthquakes and Sunrise Missions* (1983), was published, Madhubuti had started to write essays and had not published a book of poetry for twelve years. This collection is comprised of several poems that mirror earlier poems in that they demand change in and for the Black community.

The difference, however, is the lack of urgency found in these works. The poems in *Earthquakes and Sunrise Missions* are more cerebral and less spontaneous than Madhubuti's earlier poems. In this volume we find the poet working from a philosophical frame of reference, asking readers to think about their relationships with others, and to concentrate first on strengthening those relationships so that nation and institution building are possible. In "Message" there is a thoughtful voice asking the reader to work toward liberation:

> We can do what we work to do
> measure stillness and quiet
> noise is ever present.
> if we are not careful we will not
> hear the message
> when it
> arrives.
>
> (4.22-28)

These poems contain a pensive, wiser voice that does not demand, as in earlier poems, but suggests. With over twenty years of political activism, business development and teaching experience, Madhubuti is able to draw on his experiences and communicate with his readers, as in "Expectations":

> trust people
> one by one
> the darker they come
> the more you can give your heart,
> their experiences most likely are yours
>
> (2.12-16)

Though the poem essentially promotes Black unity and trust, its speaker does not shout these themes; rather, the speaker seems to offer them as suggestions for those willing to listen. It is as though Madhubuti has accepted that he will not reach everyone, that his message may not be as accepted as he once expected, but that those willing to listen can be guided toward new missions.

GroundWork: New and Selected Poems (1996) is yet another pause, like *Directionscore*, in which the poet selects certain poems from previous collections. *GroundWork* illustrates the continuation of his artistic and political evolution, as he stands thirty years after the first collection, *Think Black!*, a stronger and wiser poet/activist. Still concerned with the same tenets of the Black Arts Movement reflected in earlier works (e.g. Black economic development, social and political change through rejection of anti-Black values, etc.), he writes in the preface to *GroundWork*:

> The work here, in all of its bone-bracing energy, is the result of a life lived as a poet-activist, political person, freedom fighter, businessman, family man, and institution builder. This work should be read and understood in a historical and cultural context…. My environment is critical and essential to my understanding of the world and my (our) place in it.

The inclusion of poems that focus on Black political consciousness in *Think Black!, Black Pride, Don't Cry, Scream, We Walk the Way of the New World, Directionscore, Book of Life, Earthquakes and Sunrise Missions*, and *Killing Memory, Seeking Ancestors* reflects Madhubuti's attention to his political agenda, his understanding of the disparity Blacks face because of economic and social oppression and his need, thirty years after the first volume was published, to concentrate on the strongest messages found in those early works.

The new poems in *GroundWork* reflect his concern for a variety of themes. In "Too Many of Our Young Are Dying" he writes of the death of Black children whose lives are lost to the violence of the streets and drugs:

31

our children, in the millions
are dropping from the trees of life too soon,
their innocent hearts and bodies
are forced to navigate within modern madness
searching for life and love
in the basements of a crippled metropolis

(2.5-10)

Madhubuti indicts adults who have allowed Black children to grow up without love, to remain desperate for attention only to wander through life. He warns, "we must never stop listening to their stories & songs" (3.15).

The collection's new poems do not seem to have a specific theme or determined message, as do the earlier collections. However, they demonstrate his maturity in form and his control of language. These poems come from a wiser poet who is still passionate about empowering Black communities, but is able to deliver his messages in a more assured and stronger voice. In "Magnificant Tomorrow's" he reminds readers of the importance of Black women within the Black community:

as the women go, so go the people,
determining mission,
determining possibilities.

stopping the women stops the future.
to understand slavery, feel the eyes of mothers

(3.7-9, 4.10-11)

Furthermore, Madhubuti's subject matter in Groundwork takes him farther away from intense self-criticism. Though he wrote candidly about himself in earlier collections, the latter works reveal a more self–assured voice replacing a reactionary one; one that can accept past failures. This voice is articulated in "White People Are People Too":

> it is in me to grow
> to walk among vegetation and cultures, to think.
> it is in me to see that pain is colorless
> it is in me to value the differences of theirs.
>
> (5.24-27)

This patient speaker suggests positive action as a response to one's 'enemies', not anger or condemnation. This is a departure from the earlier poems in *Think Black!* and *Black Pride*. What one finds in *Groundwork* is a calmer speaker who has been to battle and is willing to pass on his experiences while remaining optimistic about the future.

Other themes explored in *Groundwork* and subsequent poems include family and the significance of children's safety and happiness. The last five volumes are less confrontational approach to achieving Black power and unity. These poems further reflect Madhubuti's evolution in writing style. Having risen from the role of naive young revolutionary to experienced political organizer and theorist, his art has evolved, yet still expands his original themes of Black unity and pride. He explained, "I think that in terms of skill, craft and writing, obviously you don't just stand still—you develop. I think you can look at *Ground Work* and see that all the way through.... Maturation is there. Subject matter has pretty much been the same."

The most obvious difference in these later volumes is his approach to the theme of Black nation building. Madhubuti begins to focus on the particular components of Black nation building (love, marriage, family, ancestors), instead of simply alluding to them. In the latter volumes, more emphasis is placed on specific areas readers can improve in their individual quests toward liberation. Instead of insulting "Negroes" and attacking White power structures, as in his earliest works, he discusses the harmful effects Western values can have on Black families and communities. In the poem, "A Calling," he writes: "We are short memory people, / too willing to settle for artless resumes of / rapid life brief prayers cappuccino / our young adapt to contemporary clothing without question,/as we fail to acknowledge brilliance among us" (1.1-5). He asks readers to think about their lives in profound ways so that they are equipped to change their lives. Also in these later volumes there appears to be more emphasis on the individual's personal struggle for change and direction than in earlier works.

Poems dedicated to past leaders such as Malcolm X and Hoyt Fuller, as well as legends like Gwendolyn Brooks, and poems dedicated to countries in the midst of war (e.g. Rwanda) are also found in these later works. Again, the political theorist is at work, using poetry as his vehicle to educate and inspire action among readers. In these poems, he reflects a need to remember and pay homage to great leaders of the past who will influence the future and to the great tragedies that will influence the future. In this sense, Madhubuti still acts as leader, both spiritual and cultural, in that he passes on the wisdom of the ancestors in his work, as a quieter catalyst of change.

Madhubuti shows clear signs of growth in these volumes as he continues to investigate and critique, to expose and honestly question that which stands in the way of Black unity and power. For instance, in the foreword to *Killing Memory*, he writes, "It is in poetry that I have learned to communicate best. After fourteen books published in a twenty-one year period, I have become a poet." *HeartLove: Wedding and Love Poems* (2002) is a collection of love and wedding poems. Madhubuti is still concerned with strengthening the Black family and offers readers these poems as gifts towards that goal. The collection includes meditations on commitment and love. The poems, however, are not whimsical musings. Instead, the poet investigates the complexities of relationships, offering advice and insight on what matters. In *HeartLove*, Madhubuti celebrates positive marriages, though his ultimate message is a celebration of marriage in general. The last work in the first section of the book includes an actual ceremony with parts for the minister, bride and groom, maid of honor, and best man. Here, again, is Madhubuti offering actual instructions toward achieving unity.

The second section of the book is devoted to poems about love. These poems vary from short musings on love (e.g., "The Only Time": the only time a man / can tell a woman / he loved her too much is when / he doesn't mean it") to longer pieces like "Rainforest." The natural images that are used in "Rainforest" evoke a restless spirit that longs to love and unite with a partner. The poem, like so many in this collection, is a reminder of the urgent need for Black men and women to see marriage and union as a necessary and beautiful part of nation building. Like previous works, *HeartLove* is moving, but the voice we find in these poems is not forceful or obviously clever. Instead, one hears a wise voice that warns and inspires us.

POETIC STYLE

One of the goals of many Black Arts Movement writers was to manipulate language, to own that which was used against them, and to instill new and challenging signs and symbols into the art. One must look at the use of language and form, as well as content, to truly understand the early poetry of Haki Madhubuti. From the first volume, *Think Black!* to more recent poetry in *HeartLove*, one can find significant risks in language and poetic form.

Madhubuti's early use of Black English and fusion of music and literature, along with his poetic style (signaled by his use of lower case letters and diction), mark one of the most significant components of his work, components he used in early volumes to promote messages of Black unity and power. For many Black Arts Movement artists, use of the folk vernacular was important, as it symbolized validation of Black culture, regardless of its apparent difference from mainstream White culture. For the Black Arts Movement writers, the intention was to speak to Blacks through a language with which they would most likely identify. Therefore, it was quite logical to incorporate Black English into the literature of the Movement. Madhubuti was one of many poets who advocated the use of Black language as a weapon of resistance. In *Think Black!* he states, "The Black writer learns from his people and because of his insight and 'know how' he is able to give back his knowledge to the people in a manner in which they can identify." Therefore, the use of Black English was both a stylistic choice on the part of the writer, as well as a political statement, which Madhubuti used to clearly distinguish European culture with its Standard English from Black culture with its Black English. His early poetry reflects this distinction, as he uses it to encourage Black unity and power.

Although Madhubuti seeks to communicate with the Black masses in a manner that they can understand, his poetry is only peppered with Black English and Black slang. He does not write exclusively in Black English, but rather incorporates some characteristic Black English grammar. For example, in "But He Was Cool" he writes, "wooooooooooo-jim he bes so cool" (3.16). The phrase "jim he bes" is an example of Black English grammar in which the verbal form "to be" bears the third-person present-tense suffix defying Standard European poetic forms and expectations.

Another example of Black English usage in Madhubuti's poetry is found in his abbreviation of words (e.g. "yr," "u," "blk"), separation of words with hyphens (e.g. "whi-te") and creation of new words (e.g. "yellowblack"). In doing this, he constructs a poetic style that is in line with the rich oral tradition found in African American culture, one in which language is flexible and fluid enough for the speaker to stray away from the traditional grammar and still be understood by readers. In addition, he incorporates onomatopoeic words like "KA BOM-MMM" and "BAM BAM BAM" to incite energy into the works, infusing them with sound and the fervor of the 1960s political activity. As mentioned, he begins to move toward lower case lettering with words that traditionally (according to English orthodoxy) would be capitalized. For example, he writes, "i" and "america" throughout his earlier poems in order to resist mainstream tradition and infuse his works with a new Black aesthetic.

Madhubuti's style evolves from *Think Black!* to *HeartLove* as he unapologetically uses variations of language to articulate his political and spiritual beliefs. His is a poetry that teaches as well as inspires. Thus, we find that as he moves toward a true revolutionary voice—one that presents solutions instead of merely stating problems—he moves away from fragmented words, experimental poetic forms and Black English. With *HeartLove*, Madhubuti has all but abandoned these components, opting for a more traditional style, more in line with Western poetic forms. Though his content is still focused on Black unity and power, along with love and family, he does not include the signature lower case lettering, slashes and innovative wording found in the earlier volumes.

It would be a mistake to say that Madhubuti is a better poet because he has moved away from experimental language and form. Surely this decision was a conscious one. Yet, the impact of the poems' power in *HeartLove* is strongly felt because of his move toward traditional form, hence their messages are not obscured by a somewhat self–conscious, though creative, style that marked his early work. In "Voices with Loaded Language," for instance, he writes:

> you are not really friends to me
> more like teachers, mothers, close nurturers,
> i have listened to you for twenty-three years and
> my enlargement has become quieted and determined
> reflecting your words to me.

> (1.1–5)

Here we see more attention placed on the message and the content of the poem than on the experimental style or "packaging" of the poem. The speaker's message is clearly stated, as Madhubuti's efforts are placed not so much on the explicit language of his past works but rather on the fluid and lush language he currently speaks through.

Even when he speaks of the harsh reality faced by Blacks, he is poignant, yet still more mature in his word choice. In "Volcanoes in the Souls of Children" he writes, "we have learned to sleep on bare mattresses, / we measure our tomorrows against the deaths of / eleven year olds" (1.1-3). Though he still avoids capital letters, even to represent first person pronouns, there is still an evident shift from a poetic voice that offers little to one whose wisdom is more powerful than the words used to convey it.

OTHER GENRES

In addition to his books, it is equally important to mention Madhubuti's recordings, most notably *Rise Vision Comin* (1976 and 2003) and *Medasi* (1978 and 2003). These recordings, which include music and poetry, have been re-released, finding audiences that span several generations. Their popularity amongst artists, educators and activists are a testament to the impact art has had on politics and education in the Black community. Madhubuti's recordings are the products of collaboration, which he has always maintained is essential for progress in the Black community. Through power and unity, he has consistently believed, Blacks can fulfill their missions and determine their destinies. The recent re-release of these recordings in CD form is also evidence of his understanding of the influence music has in the Black community. By reaching younger audiences through this medium, he can be as effective now as he was in the 1970s. Thus, a more experienced and wiser Madhubuti is clearly stating that the same issues that plagued the Black community in the past are still problematic now.

Despite the changes in format and style, Madhubuti's messages are still consistent. From *Think Black!* to *HeartLove*, he has remained constant in his intention to unify and empower Black people through words and to incite a revolution in the hearts and minds of Black people within the daily struggle for survival.

Toward a Theoretical Approach: The Essays

CHAPTER THREE
Toward a Theoretical Approach:
The Essays

FROM POETRY TO ESSAY

For many fans of his poetry, Madhubuti's turn toward essays was disappointing, as most only thought of him as a poet/activist. Regarding his turn toward essays and away from poetry, Madhubuti states:

> We had gone through all this pain, all this disruption, all this murder in our community. Our community had been flooded with drugs, businesses pulled out, so Book of Life for me was saying how do we hold on? How do we keep going? Poetry was very much a part of what I felt was an answer, but at the same time I knew there had to be concrete directives.

The essays gave him an opportunity to reach people in a more direct way than the poems allowed. He knew that despite the popularity of his poetry, there were concepts about Pan-Africanism and Black Nationalism that could only be expressed through prose. He stated,

41

In some sense they're [the essays] theoretical pieces, but in another sense they're not theory because they are what we've
been trying to do for the last four or five years. But I realized
too that there is a whole segment of Black people out here who
do not read poetry, may not even get to the poetry but would
pick up a book of essays.

Thus, the turn to essays was rooted in a strong desire to continue his
work as an activist/artist, to send to Black readers messages that would
empower them politically, socially, and economically.

As Madhubuti devoted his energies toward writing essays in
the early seventies, his role as activist/artist continued to evolve, ex-
pressing his growing understanding of Black Nationalism, Pan–African-
ism and political theory. As with his poetry, Madhubuti's essays
expressed his concern for the Black community through a combination
of these theories and his own solutions to the Black community's economic and social problems.

Beginning in 1971 with *Dynamite Voices: Black Poets of the
1960s* (Broadside Press), Madhubuti sought to speak through prose to
maximize his voice in the Black community and present a Black presence in literary criticism and philosophy. With *Dynamite Voices* he
sought to highlight some of the most significant Black writers of the
time, including Mari Evans, Etheridge Knight, Sonia Sanchez and Carolyn Rodgers. The book is a collection of critical essays about specific
and shared themes, styles and politics of the selected writers. In it, we
see Madhubuti move into the role of literary critic while relying on the
same passion and politics found in his poetry. In *Dynamite Voices*, he
states:

Sensibility: awareness, consciousness, fineness of feeling—
it shaped our sensibilities and shaped us…. Most of us have
been shaped by the same consciousness: a white nationalist
consciousness called Americanism that is really a refined or un-
refined, diluted version of the European colonialist sensibility.

His distinct social commentary is found in his critical essays on
fellow writers, most notably Sanchez. Of her, he writes:

Sonia Sanchez understands that the mind of the Negro works at a very conscious level; his skin tonality maintains this consciousness. Sonia enables us to move under her conscious tonality into blacker fields…. Her one word lines are like well worked sentences and her metaphors and images are those we go to sleep/wake up with for days.

In an eloquent explanation of the book's purpose, Madhubuti manages to summarize a plan for Black writers as they take Black literature in a new direction.

We plan to take one man's point of view…and try to clear up some of the misinterpretations, to show the contradictions and inconsistencies, and above all, to give direction to that body of Black poetry which exists. Hopefully, in undertaking such a task my efforts will help legitimize the Black music-lines, which are, as far as I'm concerned, already legitimate but unnoticed.

The Essays

In 1973, Madhubuti published *From Plan to Planet: Life Studies: The Need for Afrikan Minds and Institutions* (Broadside Press and Institute of Positive Education), a collection of essays aimed at informing readers of life changes they could make to motivate Black people "toward the working of and building of Afrikan minds and institutions that will deal systematically and sensibly with the problems of Afrikan people." In 1978, he moved toward publishing essays concerned with the practical political theory in *Enemies: The Clash of Races*. Both collections focus on the plans or actions advocated at the end of the poetry cycle, wherein he proposes changes in Black lifestyle and mentality as a weapon of resistance and liberation.

These collections were later followed by *Earthquakes and Sunrise Missions* (1983), which contains both essays and poetry. *Black Men: Obsolete, Single or Dangerous?* (1990), which sold over one million copies, examines the difficulties Black males face in America as they struggle to survive, despite drugs, violence and racism. *Claiming*

Earth: Race Rage, Rape Redemption: Blacks Seeking a Culture of Enlightened Empowerment was published in 1994. It includes a collection of essays that address the "culture of containment," a term Madhubuti uses to describe the results of white cultural supremacy. In 2002, he published *Tough Notes: A Healing Call for Creating Exceptional Black Men.* This book is essentially a collection of letters written to young Black men. It is Madhubuti's attempt to discuss the many issues and obstacles that influence their decisions and may keep them from becoming the men they should become.

Amiri Baraka, one of the most prolific political leaders of the 1960s, also understands the value of social literature. Baraka, along with other Black Nationalists such as Marcus Garvey, Malcolm X, Maulana Karenga and Addison Gayle, Jr., understood the importance of asserting political opinion, strategy, etc., through essays. What distinguishes Madhubuti from other Black Nationalists, however, is his focus on the socialization of Black people in the U.S. and their acceptance of a cultural revolution as a necessary step toward building a Black nation. That is, unlike Marcus Garvey, Malcolm X, Maulana Karenga and Amiri Baraka—four of the most influential Black Nationalist leaders of the twentieth century—Madhubuti's discourse is less concerned with building national political structures for Black Americans, his focus is developing their consciousness based on an African-oriented value system in order to better equip them for surviving as a nation, and as a Black minority within a white majority America. This, he wrote, could be accomplished through cultural awareness, embracing an African value system, rejecting Capitalism or Communist political ideology and building Black institutions.

The use of the social essay helped Madhubuti map out his plan for "everyday folk" who might otherwise dismiss his ideas as stated or inferred in his poetry. His goal was to lay out a plan for other Black Nationalists to identify problems and solutions that could enhance the lives of the majority of Black Americans who would remain in America. Madhubuti's idea centers on equipping Black Americans with a Black Nationalist/Pan-Africanist agenda that would prove useful in America. Unlike the early twentieth century Black political leader Marcus Garvey, who believed there was no difference between native Africans and

American Blacks, Madhubuti insists that there is a major difference: culture. Garvey's insistence that Africans and African Americans have a common bond that allows for the return of African Americans to Africa is countered, in part, by Madhubuti, who asserts that Black Americans have been alienated from their African heritage and forced to accept Western values that inherently teach them to hate all that is African. In *From Plan to Planet*, he states, "We, along with our parents and their parents, have, consciously and unconsciously, internalized the values of our oppressor [white Americans] to the point that we are himself [sic]."

It is Madhubuti's contention that certain Western values have corrupted African Americans, separating them from their African ancestry and other Blacks throughout the Diaspora, including Africa. Madhubuti's thesis in *From Plan to Planet* is focused on African Americans' acceptance of certain European value systems that have led them to regard anything that is not European as "alien to us, and considered unnatural." As a result, most Blacks reject African names, rituals, beauty aesthetics, language systems and dress, among other things. This has led, he argues, to Blacks being irresponsible, especially in their use of drugs and their acceptance of poor education. He has stated, "We have ceased to be responsible to ourselves, to our race, and to our children."

From Plan to Planet is broken into three sections that discuss topics ranging from "Life-Studies," "The Black Arts" and "Worldview." In "Worldview" he advocates the need for "Afrikan" education and maintains that Blacks' minds, lifestyle, and collective vision have all been shaped by education. He also asserts that because Europeans have re–ordered the world through brute strength and mental manipulation, African Americans must take charge of the education process their children undergo. Such criticism of Western values and the need to incorporate the Nguzo Saba (seven Swahili-based principles) are based on Maulana Karenga's Kawaida theories regarding a new value system.

In fact, Madhubuti's work does not originate new ideas concerning values systems, but relies heavily on Karenga's theories, as he applies them to his own understanding of social consciousness among Blacks. Though Karenga's The Organization US was focused on incorporating alternative values and rituals for Blacks (alternative in that they are African-based, instead of Western-based), it is clear that Madhubuti uses Karenga's concepts as a foundation for his own solutions, thus utilizing these theories as Karenga intended.

In *From Plan to Planet*, Madhubuti questions Black educators' ability to teach Black children. He writes, "It has become increasingly clear that 'Black educators' are not going to provide the direction needed to save the minds and creative spirit of our children." Therefore, Black educators must start with a Black value system that is reinforced in the homes of students. He believed this new system, again rooted in Kawaida, would empower both teacher and student, connecting both to an African-centered worldview that affirms, instead of negates, Blackness.

It is not until readers are halfway through the collection that the definition of Madhubuti's proposed "Black value system" is given. Originating from the Nguzo Saba, Madhubuti's Black value system is based on African tradition and reason. The seven principles: unity, self-determination, collective work and responsibility, cooperative economics, purpose, creativity and faith, are "absolutely necessary" for all Blacks, according to Madhubuti. He states that incorporation of these values will lead to stronger Black organizations and ultimately to Black institutions. This is also Karenga's original purpose of the principles. In *From Plan to Planet*, he states that Black nationalists "realize that we cannot totally transplant African Culture in an American context. Therefore, we must adjust our traditions to fit and facilitate our movement in America." In fact, Madhubuti refrences Karenga throughout "A Black Value System: Why the Nguzo Saba?"

Madhubuti argues throughout his essays that people are essential to nation building, and he focuses on Black people in his theories of Black Nationalism. For him, separation of Black people from Whites is essential for the survival of Blacks, as he believes America is a nation of nations, and the existence of a Black nation in America is imperative for their survival. *From Plan to Planet* marks the beginning of Madhubuti's use of the essay form to present practical lifestyle changes to Black readers. It is clear that he becomes invested in the idea that unlike poetry, the essay provides a vehicle for straightforward dialogue with readers. This first collection of essays is successful in accomplishing Madhubuti's goal of using the social essay as another means of communicating solutions to the problems Black Americans face.

In his second collection of essays, *Enemies: The Clash of Races* (1978), he abandons the strategy he employed in *From Plan to Planet*, in which he proposes simple yet necessary changes for Blacks to use in order to empower themselves and their communities. Instead, he compiles a series of essays that analyze race relations, political ideologies and European control over Blacks throughout the Diaspora. Following the tradition of other Black Nationalists, such as Baraka and Malcolm X, Madhubuti provides historical evidence and political theory to counter the negative effects of Western imperialism and racism on the lives of non-Whites. He writes passionately, often citing sources that support his claims. The work is divided into four chapter subheadings: "What It Is," "Life-Studies Two," "Struggle" and "Decisions and Movement." In *Enemies: The Clash of Races* it is clear that he wishes first to define the problems Blacks and other non-whites face, then discuss the importance of Black Nationalism as a step toward eradicating white dominance. It is equally clear that, like his first book of essays, he wishes to encourage empowerment via lifestyle changes. Finally, he proposes practical strategies toward gaining Black power and unity.

In the essay "From the Beginning: The Decision is to Fight," he uses shocking facts to enlighten Black readers of the reality of their existence. He states: "We have never been taught to think for or about ourselves or our condition. We willingly fall into the white sugar traps, and the poison, slowly, but effectively, decays our ability to subjectively question our position in the world." On education, he continues his harsh criticism of Black teachers that was first heard in *From Plan to Planet*: "Today many Black teachers are inadequate babysitters and do not possess the vision to know that those they sit with are our future." He goes on to criticize Black board members and chairs of Black Studies departments who sit "on the boards of large corporations, occupying top administrative jobs in the local, state and federal governments, serving as vice-presidents of trade unions, etc." Such characters, he warns, will do the Black community harm because they are only interested in promoting their own selfish agendas, not serving as liaisons for the Black community.

While many of the essays in *Enemies* touch on the same subject matter as those in *From Plan to Planet*, Madhubuti's range as an essayist is more pronounced. He incorporates more outside sources to support his claims and provides more complex ideologies about race relations and white imperialism. In addition, he challenges the intellectual community (both Black and white) over the "rights" of certain groups to dominate others. He states that the "liberation of Black people will express itself in many ways, but we see some of the most tangible and workable ways at this time as Nationalism, Pan-Africanism and African Communism." From there Madhubuti defines each political concept, stating afterward, "Our culture must be traditionally based, yet at the same time must meet the needs of a highly scientific and technological world future."

Through historical overview of Black Nationalism, dating back to the Slave Era, Madhubuti poses the following question: How do we defeat White supremacy and at the same time survive and develop for the benefit of Black people? He further states, "The ideology of White Supremacy disguises itself in systems such as Capitalism, Communism, Socialism, Racism, Imperialism, Christianity, Islam, etc., as perpetuated and practiced by the white race." Therefore, Blacks do not need reactionary theory, but instead "affirmative theory," which is at the root of Black Nationalism. Furthermore, it is in this collection of essays that Madhubuti splits with other Black Nationalists who turn toward communism in their quest for Black liberation.

In 1974, he departed from Amiri Baraka's Congress of African Peoples, which began to advocate a Communist ideology. Though Baraka and Madhubuti seem to be in accord concerning their concepts of Black Nationalism, they ultimately stand opposed on the issue of Communism. Baraka writes in his "Coordinator's Statements" that, "We are controlled largely by the ideas of our oppressors. The political party [Congress of African People] must build alternative systems, values, institutions that will move and raise us."

This distrust of leftist politics is echoed in Madhubuti's theses in both *From Plan to Planet* and *Enemies*. However, he also wrote, "The white left is more dangerous than the white right because we know exactly where the white right stands." In addition, he points out that Marx and Engels were both pro-slavery in that they believed nothing accomplished throughout history could have been accomplished without slavery. Thus, he ponders how Communism could be a viable option for the Black struggle. He points to two organizations: the African Liberation Support Committee and the Congress of African People. Both organizations were "infiltrated" by the white left and thus significantly affected by their ideologies.

Madhubuti discussed his major concern with Leftist politics as part of Black liberation when he stated:

> The Marxist position is that white racism…is a result of the profit motive brought on by the European slave trade and that white racism or anti-Black feelings didn't exist before such time. . .yet, one of the major facts of history is that white racism preceded and advanced itself thousands of years before European capitalism and imperialism was even systematically conceived.

This was an indictment against not only Communists that tried to influence the Black Liberation Movement (and certainly some were successful), but also those Blacks who became Communists in the name of Black liberation. Hence, the conflict between Baraka and Madhubuti concerning Leftist theories became a key issue when Madhubuti left the Congress of African People. Upon reflection, Madhubuti stated:

> During this period we had these real battles, this ongoing battle with these lefties. You had a whole segment of the Black left trying to make us Black left and trying to get us to work with these White lefties. You got a whole segment of the Black revolutionary community, mainly the Panther Party, trying to get us to work with these white lefties…. Here we were going on with a Nationalist Pan-Africanist program. It was never, we felt, anything other than trying to rebuild these communities.

This split with Baraka's national organization signaled a beginning for Madhubuti to separate himself from many Black Nationalists whose turn toward leftist theories marked a change in Black political organizations. Yet Madhubuti resisted these changes, stating in *Enemies* that "Capitalist integration and communist integration have at their centers the same controlling mechanism; white people. Why do some of our former Black Nationalist [sic] now fight so feverishly for "alliances," "coalitions" and "associations" with the same whites who have been documented in blood not to be just our enemy but the enemy to the living world?"

In 1983, Madhubuti published *Earthquakes and Sunrise Missions*, a collection of poetry and essays. This work, published eleven years after his first collection of essays, *From Plan to Planet*, again critiques Blacks' condition in the Western world, and proposes changes in lifestyle and mentality. He questions the aggressive nature of Whites in this book and points to their ability to execute their worldview above all others. For him, this explains the dominance of White values throughout the world, particularly amongst African Americans. It is not that Blacks do not have a value system of their own (one based on African concepts and traditions); indeed, the problem lies in Blacks' inability to practice such systems within a Western context.

In the Afterword of this collection, noted literary critic Darwin Turner states, "It is as though Madhubuti has chosen to move from the role of virtuoso performer and to assume more often the role of artistic, prophetic educator." As a result, *Earthquakes* is a departure from earlier works, in which Madhubuti's voice becomes more compassionate and less anxious than the voice in his early poetry. He seeks understanding, rather than simply condemnation, even of "Negroes" who are consumed with capitalist dreams and ambition. It is interesting to note that *Earthquakes and Sunrise Missions* was published after Madhubuti earned a Masters of Fine Arts in Creative Writing at the University of Iowa, where he also taught in the African American Studies Department that was chaired by Turner, who took a strong stand on the importance of adding literary criticism to the growing number of publications by Black Arts Movement writers. The suggestions in this collection also show the influence of African-centered ideologies in Madhubuti's life. His work is influenced by several Black Nationalist organizations, such as the Nation of Islam and The Shrine of the Black Madonna Pan-African Orthodox Christian Church, which promotes a proactive approach to Christianity in its followers, thereby encouraging them to work toward social and spiritual liberation.

By the early 1990s, Madhubuti was still working toward Black liberation through his publishing company, the independent schools he co-founded with his wife, his position as a professor at Chicago State University (as well as founder and director of its Gwendolyn Brooks Center), and his role as father and husband. His poetry was highly anthologized, and his essays were still in publication. However, he began to turn his efforts toward a new theme, one that would bring him closer to a new audience—college-age Black men who, whether in college or not, were at risk because of rampant violence, drug use and stereotypes that seemed to render them close to extinction.

Black Men: Obsolete, Single, Dangerous? features a collection of essays in which Madhubuti explores the plight of Black men and their future in a country which seems to care nothing about their deaths or their existence. He writes of "young Black men in their late twenties or early thirties living in urban America, lost and abandoned, aimlessly walking and hawking the streets with nothing behind their eyes but anger" (preface). These men, he finds, are lost because of several factors: economic status, residential segregation, education, institutional oppression, political participation (or lack of it), crime, health, and child and family issues. This collection's central theme is in line with his previous works, which examine the economic, social and cultural effect Western values have had on Black people. He suggests that young Black men are victims of not only racism, but the Black community's lack of concern and direction, a message found throughout his work written during the late 1960s to late 1970s.

In *Black Men*, Madhubuti focuses his attention on the street corner, the common hang out spot for so many urban Black males. He points to the lack of cultural understanding or appreciation on the part of these youths as a reason they are lost. To explain Black males' anger and distrust, he also points to the importance of culture in a community. As stated in his earlier essays, he believes that culture is an abstract idea to most of these young men. As a result, they have nothing to ground their consciousness in, except the materialism and anti-Black male messages they receive daily in media images and scholarly rhetoric. He explained, "A people's consciousness, the way they view and operate in the world, is shaped by their (or another's) culture."

Furthermore, this lack of understanding Black culture and nurturance of it has led to a survival/dependency attitude amongst Blacks that "breeds people who riot, rather than plan progressive change or revolution." Madhubuti uses his Black Nationalist stance from the social essays written in the 1970s to analyze the problems Blacks face in the 1990s. In addition to the discussion of culture, Madhubuti points to the lack of male role models within the Black community. He also looks at the importance of Black male/female relationships, stating, "the root...of Black life is in the relationship established between Black men and women in a white supremacist system.... Sound and loving relationships are the core of a sane, happy and fruitful life." He also points to the lack of power Black men possess, given the fact that most do not own land nor do they have a lot of money, and that their manhood is measured by such acquisitions. This, in turn, affects their relationships with Black women since they often cannot "deliver the 'American dream.'" The book suggests that a great deal of the problems facing young Black men are rooted in the effect of white Western culture's influence regarding values in Black communities. Again, we see Madhubuti return to the ideas he stated in his earlier essays and his poetry, in which he blames, among other things, a Western value system for negatively impacting Blacks socially and politically.

In the essays in *Claiming Earth*, one sees the author asking difficult questions of the Black community, questions that require internal evaluation and collective confession. He asks, for instance, "When do we call destruction our own?" in "Rape: the Male Crime (On Becoming Anti-Rapist)." Madhubuti poses a difficult challenge for Black men: "...[W]e men, as difficult as it may seem, must view all women...as extended family." He insists that internal rebuilding in the Black community requires that we "challenge tradition and cultural ways of life that relegate women to inferior status in the home, church/mosque/temple, workplace, political life, and education."

The essays in *Claiming Earth* are divided into five chapters: "Culture and Race," "The Genius of Deep Reflection/The Quality of Change," "Who Owns the Earth?" "Sunlight in the West" and "Beginnings and Findings." Each reflects his understanding of what is needed to restore faith and love in not only Black American communities, but throughout the Diaspora. His political insight fuels the fire in these essays, particularly when he speaks of Haiti and Rwanda. The inclusion of non-American Black communities is a direct result of his Pan-Africanist conviction which, by the time *Claiming Earth* was published, had been tested and energized from trips to Africa and his association with others who saw Pan-Africanism as a viable political ideology. Three trips to Africa in the 1970s, including Nigeria, Senegal and Tanzania, led to a name change (from Don L. Lee to Haki R. Madhubuti) as well as a deeper understanding of African consciousness and the importance of this consciousness in the liberation of Africans throughout the Diaspora.

In addition to writing essays, Madhubuti has edited important works, including *Why L.A. Happened* (1993) and *The Million Man March: Day of Absence* (1993), which gathers comments by his contemporaries on two important events in African American history: the Los Angeles riots and Nation of Islam leader Louis Farrakhan's Million Man March on Washington, D.C. His involvement as editor and publisher is further evidence of his commitment to empowering Blacks and unifying Black political power. Both collections include essays by noted intellectuals such as Cornell West and political activists, including Jesse Jackson.

The most recent collection of essays, *Tough Notes: A Healing Call for Creating Exceptional Black Men* (2002), continues his investigation of the Black male presence that he began in *Black Men: Obsolete, Single, Dangerous?* This work, however, speaks directly to men of various ages and experiences. In it, Madhubuti is concerned with reaching Black men to remind them of their responsibilities to their families, communities and nation. He states, "All of my reflections throughout this book have a common theme—the making of exceptional men." He also addresses issues concerning money, relationships and education, among others.

In "Vision: Young Professionals Must Step Up," he suggests that a Black American Congress is needed to help shape and assert a national agenda that serves Black Americans, and mentions the need for strong leadership and accountability on the part of young professionals, who must understand their responsibility within the Black community.

These later books are still not far removed from his earlier political and social ideologies. For instance, Madhubuti states, "Self–determination must be fundamental in our thoughts and actions," it is obvious that the Kawaida principles are still part of his theoretical foundation.

Clearly the social essay, as seen in the past by other Black activists, has placed Madhubuti's Black Nationalist ideology in the hands of readers more familiar with his poetry. This form affords him the chance to detail solutions that were proposed in his poetry, solutions that are embedded in a Pan–African ideology that demands change on the part of Black people. Keeping in line with his Black unity/power theme, these essays illustrate Madhubuti's ability to analyze complex political theory, while maintaining his role as a community advocate, as opposed to a political organizer.

Further, he ends with a call to Black men to build Black independent institutions and warns them to avoid giving their lives to Fortune 500 companies. Instead, he suggests, they should devote their lives to saving their communities. With this collection, he is able to reflect on his experiences, while still inspiring readers to take action that is positive and uncompromising. From the chapter on naming children to the chapter on affirmative action, *Tough Notes* does not apologize; instead it demands of its readers a serious examination of their lives and purpose.

Ultimately, his essays, like his poetry, are evidence of his commitment to the Black Arts Movement's original goals: empower Black people through art, replace Western aesthetics with a Black aesthetic as a reference for judging Black art, and become politically active in order to work toward rebuilding community through strengthening families and Black institutions. Haki Madhubuti managed to accomplish these objectives during the Black Arts Movement, and he continues to work in accord with these objectives years after it.

Personal
Choices

CHAPTER FOUR
Personal Choices

Haki Madhubuti has emerged from the Black Arts Movement as one of the most influential writers/activists, using his art as a weapon in the fight for Black liberation. He has maintained a strong Black Nationalist, Pan-Africanist political stance, one which reflects the efforts of other vanguards of the Black Power Movement and his own ideas concerning Black empowerment. More important, Madhubuti proves that many of the goals and objectives of the Black Power and Blacks Arts Movements were attainable. That is, it is possible for Black people to be creative, love their culture and other Black people, reject many Western values deemed destructive to the Black identity and stand against capitalism and other political systems, while proposing new ones that benefit all people, not just Whites.

Specifically, Madhubuti's consistency is found in five areas: using art to instill positive images and ideas into Black culture, working as an educator to influence Black youth, building institutions that provide economic direction and security for Black neighborhoods, building a strong family as a husband and father and searching, as a political, cultural and community intellectual, for new and innovative ideas that will benefit his community.

As detailed in chapter 3, Madhubuti's early poetry reveals various phases of his evolution that mark his development from an anti-white poet who was more reactionary than revolutionary, to a cultural stabilizer who is able to provide solutions for the concepts and practices he so keenly identifies as enemies of Black liberation. He has clearly surpassed so many of his colleagues in this regard, publishing twenty-seven books to date and winning many awards, including the National Endowment for the Arts Award, the National Endowment for the Humanities Award, the American Book Award, and the Gwendolyn Brooks Distinguished Poets Award.

Furthermore, Madhubuti chose to work as an educator, and a professor at an urban college (Chicago State University) despite many offers to teach at larger, predominantly white institutions. His role as co-founder of several African-centered schools in Chicago is also part of his commitment to improving educational opportunities for Black children. Though many of Madhubuti's peers also supported the need for quality education in the Black community, the majority were not willing to open schools as part of their commitment. His Institute of Positive Education has been operating for over thirty years. When asked about the success of the school, he stated:

> The school basically started as our answer to how do we impact young people in this community in a way in which we stimulate them to be better than they think they can be and most certainly better than the way people outside of this community think they can become. But at the same time, we wanted to try to deal with what we called African–centered education. That was education based upon values that were centered on extended family.

Madhubuti has also held true to his commitment to building institutions that provide economic power to the Black community. Through his work at Third World Press, now forty years old, he has been able to publish not only his own work, but the work of Black writers who may have been rejected by the larger white-owned publishing companies. Third World Press is now one of the oldest Black-owned independent press in the county. It boasts a roster of writers and editors including Gwendolyn Brooks, Gloria Naylor, Tavis Smiley, Amiri Baraka and Chancellor Williams.

Futhermore, his administrative offices and schools are housed in multi-million dollar structures and in Black neighborhoods on Chicago's South Side. Though he could afford office suites downtown, Madhubuti chooses to stay "in the community" in order to serve as a model for other Black entrepreneurs. He has stated:

> At one point, I cannot only look at my books, I can look at all these other books. I can look at these structures, these institutions that are ours [they own a half of a block on Chicago's South Side]. So nobody tells me what to do or not do [sic]. What to publish or not to publish. I'm probably one of the freest Black men alive.

He goes on to explain the importance of family in the Black community:

> I see that in terms of trying to build our communities…I don't see them being built without families…. And I think these commitments have to be made and [that] they have to be lasting…even if we'd built these institutions and I didn't have a family, then it seems that there is a certain amount of failure.

Throughout his essays, he reiterates this point about the Black family as a vital part of the Black community. Black men, he reminds readers in *Black Men: Obsolete, Single, Dangerous?* must be role models not only for their children, but for younger Black men in the community who will one day occupy the role of father (many before they graduate high school).

In his personal life, he has worked and still works hard to maintain a strong family rooted in love, trust and responsibility. He takes his role as husband and father very seriously. He has five children—Shabaka, Mariama, Bomani, Akili and Laini—and has been happily married to his wife, Safisha, for thirty years. He has stated: "I don't see life without children, without family. I don't buy into the lonely artist, the writer, the painter, the musician."

His relationship with his wife, is a testament to his belief that many Black women are true family and community leaders. As a result, he supports his wife's career and personal goals, taking on more responsibility at home and working with her at the Institute of Positive Education. His wife, Dr. Safisha Madhubuti (Dr. Carol D. Lee), is an associate professor in the School of Education at Northwestern University and is chair of the board at the Betty Shabazz International Charter School. She is one of the most respected scholars of education in the country and one of the few who has actually built and maintained independent educational institutions.

As we continue to progress through the twenty first century, the conditions under which Blacks live will continue to change and, with hope, improve, as increased access to higher education and political offices affords more Blacks positions of power. Haki Madhubuti will remain active as an artist, entrepreneur, educator, political activist and family man. His life and work are inspirational to many who were disillusioned at the end of the Black Arts Movement, seeing it as a failure, instead of a triumph. He remains a vanguard whose vision of Black liberation still propels him on to develop more institutions and further develop those he founded years ago (e.g. Chicago State University's Gwendolyn Brooks Center and the Gwendolyn Brooks Annual Writer's Conference).

Madhubuti has stated that he is planning to expand Third World Press by publishing new writers, and he has plans to include more novelists. He published his memoir, *YellowBlack: The First Twenty-One Years Of A Poet's Life*, and is working on a collection of essays and a work of fiction. When asked about his life and work, he stated:

> It seems to me that if you believe in something, you give it all you've got. You don't hold nothing back. You don't hold nothing back. You just go to the edge of the cliff and just give it all. And if you're doing what is right, you're not going to fall over the cliff. And that's where we are.

CHAPTER FIVE

The
Interview

CHAPTER FIVE
The Interview

Lita: Why do you think more scholarly research has not been done on your work?

Haki: Why do I feel it's not amazing that more has not been done on my work?

Lita: Yes.

Haki: As a Pan-African Nationalist who has not spent a lot of time on rhetoric, but who has taken the values, the theories, the ideological positions and made them reality, that means two things: one, that I am not involved in a lot of self-promotion; two, at least two or three of the programs that we decided to give our lives to required so much time that, one, I'm not out making a lot of friends in the sense of "politicing," okay, two, out of the writers and poets to emerge out of the 60s and have essentially made a major contribution, I'm the only one who has not been published by white publishers—not at all—with the exception of when Blacks do anthologies or stuff like that. All of my books, 100 percent of my books, have been published by Black publishers. Therefore my relationship in many cases with white media, and some cases with Black media, is not the same as other writers who one would consider my peers.

Obviously, Nikki Giovanni and I came along at the same time. I had published before Nikki and in fact helped her get her first book published. But she decided very early that she wanted to move into the mainstream. And I decided to stay with Broadside Press and stay with the "Blackstream." Now, I also think this position that we take is frightening to a lot of people. It's frightening because often they're looking in and they want to leave this community. It's one thing to be at a Black university or a university where there are a number of Black students, or even be in Black studies or African American Studies, and talk this stuff. But it's really a threat at one level and I don't understand why. Any people who are in control of their own cultural imperatives… are about the perpetuation, the development, the survival of themselves.

And I've always felt that I've been given a gift in terms of poetry. And the poetry has informed my life and has allowed me to get to this point. I wouldn't be here without the poetry, no doubt about that. I'm primarily a poet. But I learned from Gwendolyn Brooks, Hoyt Fuller, Dudley Randall, Margaret and Charlie Burroughs, and even Langston Hughes and Sterling Brown, to a certain extent, that essentially we can do more than we do. But in order to do that you've got to work. It takes a long time to write a good poem. It takes an awful lot of time to write a great poem, if we ever get to that point. But when you have a community that is under siege, what else do you do? Sure I'm saying the poetry has contributed, but I think that the building of the schools and running the press and bookstores at one time also have contributed substansially.

I think that the great majority of my work has been in the Black community, not tangential to it, not in other circles, but in the Black community. And I think when you make that kind of commitment, you automatically cut yourself off from people writing about you, from people basically saying, okay, this is good work, let's try to highlight it, from all kind of awards, all different friendships. I can go all the way down the line.

Lita: You touched on a few things that I'm going to ask you about in more detail later. I'm going to start out with your early years. If you could just describe your family background—birth date, where you grew up, what kind of family you grew up in, neighborhood, things of that nature.

Haki: I was born in Little Rock, Arkansas, February 23, 1942. I don't know if my mother and father were married. They didn't stay together long enough for me to even question him about it. And I never asked my mother. We left Little Rock—I do know this. When I was born, my mother was by herself. I don't know if I was born in a hospital or at home. But I do know that my father was not there and that became his history, not being there. As a result of that, I was not named after him. I was just given a name. I don't know where Don came from. The L stands for Luther. I was named after my grandfather. And of course, Lee was my father's name.

Anyway, they left and went to Michigan. And I don't know if they went to Detroit first or outside of Detroit. Following the acts of my father, he was basically a hustler. I've never known him to work for anybody, especially white people, but he was into gambling and anything in the street. He played trombone for a while.

And I don't know too much of the history of my early life, other than that my mother and father did not stay together. And shortly after my sister was born, her name was Jacklyn; my mother and father separated. And by that time we were in Detroit. So it still had to be in the forties.

What I remember in terms of my early days, I write about a little bit in *Claiming Earth* in the chapter on intellectual development. I just remember my mother working all the time. And I saw very early that school and the development of my mind were exciting. And I've always been somewhat into books. But I found school—elementary school, high school—to be somewhat of an escape, because shortly after, we moved to Detroit. My mother was not a skilled person. I don't think she finished high school. I do know for certain that she could read and write. But the jobs she could find—understand that we were living under legal apartheid in America; it's still the 1940s, so employment for Black women was really very limited. And she would do everything she could to maintain our family—day work, sell her body, to cashier in the grocery store. I remember this very clearly because I write about it—that we lived in this apartment building that was owned by a Negro preacher.

He was a big preacher in town because he not only owned that apartment building, but he also had a funeral home and he was a minister. I don't remember his name; I'm sure I could find it if I researched it. He was basically going with my mother. We were living in the basement of this apartment building. But going with her was not enough—she had to actually janitor for that apartment building. One of the most painful times of my life was basically seeing her carrying these garbage cans all three stories. I'm saying she always worked. And he was a very violent and jealous man, and he would beat her up regularly. Finally, we got out of the situation.

We moved out, but she moved into another situation that was just as damaging and dangerous. She became a barmaid at Sunny Wilson's in Detroit, which was one of the better bars for the Negro community at the time. And being so pretty, she attracted the fastest and the worst of men. Eventually we moved again, and she hooked up with a brother. His name was Chester Givens. He worked at Ford Motor Company. And they began to live together and he became kind of our stepfather. They didn't marry. I'm pretty sure of this because we didn't take his name and she didn't take his name.

We always lived in basically apartments. At that time they were tenements. And even though he went to work everyday, he was an alcoholic, and by that time I'm pretty sure she met him while she was working in the sex trade. However, she stopped working, probably because of his insistence. But she was hooked on drugs and alcohol at that point. And it was just holy hell in terms of me and my sister. So by that time I was in high school, and life was just very, very difficult because she had to feed her habit and eventually alcohol went into drugs. And in order to feed her habit, she eventually ended up prostituting herself. And there were many nights, especially on weekends, when I'd go out looking for my mother. She'd be in a hotel with someone and I would just try to find her.

Obviously this affected me in a very negative way, and essentially what it did to me was it put me inside a shell. The escape for me at that point was basically music. The Motown sound had hit, and I had played the trumpet in grade school and high school and was trying to become a musician. It is an interesting part of my life because being very thin and this color. I got my clothes from the Chinese laundry and the Salvation Army. We never got anything new. I really can't remember ever going to buy new clothes. We lived in extreme poverty. Part of the poverty had to do with poverty of spirit. Normally, because my stepfather worked at Ford Motor Company, he'd have a decent salary. But he just drank it up.

I could deal with it to a certain level, but it had a disastrous effect on my sister. She was the last born, and she looked a lot like my mother, and she was very spoiled. We all looked out for her, but there wasn't any kind of quality nurturing. And because of what was happening to my mother all saneness was gone from our lives. She ended up getting pregnant at the age of fourteen years old. And this was back in the 1950s, so it's not like today where it's like "so what?" It was a major event, and it really hurt everybody, especially me. Of course, I went out looking for the man who had done it and that turned into a rather bloody situation. But the point is that shortly after she was pregnant, my mother went out and overdosed. It was a very nasty thing. In fact, she had been molested, raped and beat up real bad, to the point where we couldn't even open the casket at the funeral.

So at that point, my sister had her first child. I was around sixteen. And I had already gotten into music pretty deeply. I was pretty good on the trumpet and was trying to write music. And obviously I was influenced a great deal by Miles Davis and Louis Armstrong. He[Miles Davis] was the coolest thing at that point. Although I did realize that the better trumpet player at that time was Louis Armstrong. He was also at that time the all–American trumpet player. And his public demeanor was somewhat embarrassing to progressive people. I did not realize until much later on that that was just Louis Armstrong. It wasn't that he was necessarily trying to ingratiate himself to white people. That was just the humanity of the man. It was just how powerful he was in terms of his humanity and his musicianship.

Understand that my father at that point was never really in our lives. He never contributed to the family. The only time I ever remember him doing anything for my sister and I was when he bought me a suit. I got that suit and I was so embarrassed. Of course, I didn't wear the damned thing. It just hurt. But it hurt me more that my sister didn't really get what she wanted. At that point, it really crystallized for me that in the final analysis, I was going to have to depend on myself. I was going to have to do something.

I just took a Greyhound bus and came to Chicago. I stayed with an aunt for a while and then I moved to the YMCA on Fiftieth and Michigan. And I went to Dunbar High School. I finished Dunbar, did a two-year program in one year. I came out of Dunbar and couldn't find a job. And I tried to join the Air Force here in Chicago, but I had a heart murmur and was rejected. They actually gave me a slip of paper and said, "Take this to your draft board and you won't have to worry about going to the military." But being a young man, I was just hurt and said, "Okay, what are you going to do now?" I didn't really have family because the family had more or less ostracized us because of my mother. There was never any older family, other than my mother's sister, that really helped us.

So I guess in terms of the early part of life, that was it until high school. I came out of Dunbar, couldn't find a job. Joined the magazine selling group, which was advertised in the *Defender* [Newspaper]. You know: "MAKE YOUR LIFE IN SALES." Basically a Black man and woman got a couple of cars and got a contract with these magazines—*Life, Time, Jet, Ebony*—whatever magazines were out there at that time. And we would sell these subscriptions. So they would gather together all these young teenagers and we'd just travel in these cars to these small towns and go door to door, knocking on doors trying to sell subscriptions, lying about trying to work our way through the university. And the only thing I can say good about this is that it was the first time that the thought of higher education ever entered my mind.

One thing I failed to mention, which was critical to my early development, around thirteen years old, my mother had asked me to go to a library to check out a book by Richard Wright. And the title of the book was *Black Boy*. You must understand that at that time, this whole question of identity was never a large part of my consciousness. In the Black community you still had white is right, yellow is mellow, brown is fine and Black step back. And so we were still in that kind of ethos, which was really tearing the community apart. It was certainly tearing me apart, because I didn't understand what was happening.

We lived in the final years of my mother's life right next door to the largest and most influential Black Congregational Church in Michigan. The people who went to that church didn't live in that community. It was a church that Blacks bought because the white people had moved out. They had obviously bought this church and it was a magnificent structure. But the community around the church had basically decayed: Plymouth Congregational Church.

Although my mother would take us to church, there was never any regular going. And most certainly once she got deep into the alcohol thing. But we never went to the church next door. So one day, I decided that I was going. I just wanted to meet the people in there. So I put on my little used sports coat and used pants and it was just very painful the way the kids treated me. I was introduced to a level of cruelty among upper-class Black children that I've never forgotten.

So here I go to the library to get this book *Black Boy*, and my self-esteem is very low. Obviously we don't have anything. So I didn't want to go to the library, because I didn't want to go anywhere asking for anything Black. I was ashamed of Black. But my mother prevailed, and I went and found the book on the shelf myself because I didn't want to ask the white librarian for *Black Boy*. I went to the young people's section of the library and began to read.

And for the first time in my life I was really just struck by words that propelled me into another arena. Richard Wright's *Black Boy* was so much like my own life in terms of just struggle. It was just struggle all the time. It's like you're forced to be a man when you haven't hit boyhood yet. You're forced to be a man when you haven't even become a teenager yet. And so, it just kind of gave me another insight in terms of "Wow, I'm not the only one in this mess." I never had a large running group of boys I ran with, because for me I was always someplace else. I did not find fascination in the streets. I did not find fascination doing what boys did. I was not athletic.

I read most of *Black Boy* that day at the library, then checked it out and read the rest that evening. So it really kind of propelled me into another whole area of thinking. After I took that back, I checked out his *Uncle Tom's Children, Native Son,* and *Twelve Million Black Voices.* Eventually I read everything that Wright had written and began to study his life in terms of the impact of politics on his life.

My first introduction to the whole Communist Movement was through his essay in a collection where he talks about how Communism had failed intellectuals, "The God That Failed." It's a very important essay and gave me some insight into politics, at least left politics. This is why, at one point, I've never been pulled into the left like a lot of our intellectuals are. I understood clearly what Wright went through in terms of trying to be an artist. But I went through everything Wright wrote. He was a poet, too. Not his major area of writing, but he did write poetry. His work started my long journey toward literature in terms of reading. Through Wright I came in contact with Langston Hughes, Claude McKay and a lot of the early Renaissance writers and writers of his generation, Wright's generation. You know, Melvin B. Tolson, Margaret Walker Alexander and, of course, eventually, Gwendolyn Brooks. And that started my whole literary thing.

And to bring this to some conclusion, I got very sick, I think, in East St. Louis. The people I was traveling with left me in the hotel. They just left. All I had with me was my trumpet, flugelhorn, my one suit, the first new suit I'd ever had that I got for my mother's funeral. My overcoat, two or three shirts, underwear, socks, suitcase, slide ruler (I thought I was going to be a mathematician at one time.) They just left me. And so this brother had given me the twenty dollars 'cause I hadn't really made anything selling these magazines. So I paid my bill and went over to St. Louis and joined the Army.

I had already begun to read. Even when I was traveling I had a few books with me. I had my books, my music, and a slide ruler. So I decided I was going to join the Army. I hadn't taken this waiver from the Air Force, so I knew what the problem was—I had a heart murmur. So I decided that I didn't want to go into the regular Army. I just wanted to go into the Reserves. If I could just get six months, you know, get some weight on me, get some food, three meals a day, regularly get a place to sleep. I'm just looking for a safety net to get on my feet.

So I go to try to join the Reserves in Missouri, but they weren't taking any reserves. They were only taking what they called the regular Army, which meant that I had to commit for three years. So I didn't have any alternative at that point. I said, "Yes, I'll try that." Getting in wasn't any problem. I had graduated from high school; I'd graduated from Dunbar here (in Chicago). And you know I was considered pretty intelligent. In fact, I had scored high enough for Officers Candidate School. But I wasn't thinking about being an officer.

So what happened when we had the physical in this large room with all these white doctors? You know, most of these doctors were white and working on their medical degree via the military. So they were young. So I just went to the youngest doctor there, and when he got to checking my heart, asked me to do some push ups and stuff like that, he asked me, "What's wrong with your heart?" I said, "There's nothing wrong with my heart. I'm just nervous. I haven't been around this many white people in my life." I got in the Army.

Lita: (Laughter) That explained the murmur, huh?

Haki: Uh–huh. He just missed it.

Lita: Now, in terms of, I guess until about the time you entered the Army, did you have, and this might go back to reading Wright's work, did you have any understanding in terms of race and class?

Haki: Yes. Sure. Reading Wright most certainly touched on race and class, especially in *Native Son* and to a certain extent *Black Boy*. He was basically dealing with the peasant class then. In *Native Son* you're dealing with the whole urban situation so the class and economic thing just plays very heavily in that. Absolutely. However, it was not necessarily an overriding motivating factor in my life. I mean I had a very elementary understanding of what was happening. I understood then that we, being Black folks, are in a very disadvantaged position in this country. And that nothing was fair in terms of economics, in terms of politics, education. That not only were we Black, we were poor, too. So we had all these strikes against us. So I knew that whatever I ended up doing, or we ended up doing, was going to require an awful lot of work, a lot of struggle. I was very clear about this early. In terms of just seeing how my mother died and what she had to go through just to make a living for my sister and I. It was just very clear to me that it is never going to be easy. So I never expected an easy ride or a free ride at all.

So I was aware. Now, obviously, once I got into the military, my consciousness was expanded, because for the first time in my life I was receiving a regular monthly salary. I had a place to sleep. I was eating regularly. I had medical care. The work was very elementary. It was not ever taxing. At that point I just expanded my mind. I used three years of the military basically to read everything I could get my hands on about Black folks. That's what I did for three years, for two years and ten months. And once I came out of the military I had read practically everything in print on or about Black folks. I was reading somewhere close to a book a day. From that point on, nothing could stop me. From that point on, I began to accumulate a library. I was just seventeen or eighteen years old and decided I was going to have a serious library of Black literature.

Lita: Did you want to write at that point?

Haki: I was writing at that point. See what happened at basic training changed my life to a great deal. I write about this a little bit in *Claiming Earth*. When I got into basic training I was reading Paul Robeson. By that time, I had gone through Wright. I had gone through a great deal of W.E.B. Du Bois. Du Bois introduced me to Robeson, and I had gone through E. Franklin Frazier. I was reading a lot of sociology and stuff like that. So at that age, my mind never went to sleep. I was always reading.

I was on the way to basic training reading *Here I Stand* by Paul Robeson, which is his memoir. I got off the bus and the drill sergeant sees Paul Robeson's big Black magnificent face on the cover and snatches the book out of my hand. You know, barking in my face saying, "What are you doing reading this Negro communist?" That was the first time I'd heard a double negative used so creatively. [Pause] That's right he said, "Black communist." That's what it was, not Negro communist. He said "Black communist." At the same time he snatched my book, he said, "All you women up against the bus." Now there aren't any women there, just men. This is 1960. So we jump up against the bus. There are only three Black men, the rest white, and he held my book over his head and began to tear the pages out of my book and gave a page to each of the recruits telling him to use it as toilet paper. That's what he told them.

So I'm standing up against this bus, now I'm saying, "Why in the hell am I here? What am I doing in this place?" So I just decided four things that morning that would stay with me for the rest of my life:

One, I would never again, ever apologize for being Black. I am who I am, and if somebody's got a problem with that, that's their problem, it's not my problem. And if literature has taught me anything, it is that essentially you have to always go sub-surface, you have to go deep within yourself in order to be comfortable with yourself.

The second thing is that if I'm going to take this position, I have to know who I am. And so I decided I was going to put myself on my own re-education program. And this re-education program required me to re-read and to read everything that was available on, by or about Black folks.

Three that if I'm going to contribute, then not only must I read, but I must write. And I began to write. Every book I finished, I wrote a 250 word essay on the book. Now it may have been 200 words, 300 words, but my goal was to write 250 words on every book. What I recognized very early was that I did not have any serious writing skills, especially reading the quality work and then trying to write about it. So it was very good, especially at a young age, that I began to see that I had to begin to augment my writing skills. I had to learn how to write if I was going to become a writer and in order to do the work justice that I'm reading, I have to be able to write intelligently about it. So I began to study writing.

The fourth thing is that for the first time in my life—see, when he told us to get up against this bus I'm trying to figure out what my options are. Do I leave? Go AWOL? What do I do? But I was reading, luckily. This is why literature is so important. I was reading also John Oliver Killens's *And Then We Heard The Thunder*, which is a very important book about Black men in European War World II. What John Killens taught me is that when you are outnumbered you just keep your mouth shut. You think about your future. You try to strategize, etc. And that's what I did.

So I decided the fourth thing: if the ideas in Paul Robeson's book frightened this man so much he never read the book, I'm certain of that—But Paul Robeson, the man, he'd just come out of HUAC, the House of Un-American Activities Committee hearings. You got this whole Communist scare; you got the cold war being initiated. Robeson had been called before the HUAC, like Du Bois, Langston Hughes and so forth. And so, what I decided that cold morning was that if the ideas in that book that he'd never read, but most certainly the idea of Robeson, frightened him so much that I decided that I was going to go in the idea business. I'm not going to buy into picking no Goddamned cotton, carrying no garbage for White folks. That I'm going to sharpen my mind. And I didn't need anyone to legitimize it. But I'm going to sharpen my mind to the point where it will be my major weapon. And that's what I've been trying to do all my life.

Once in the military, the library became just as important as water, food and women. That's what was important. I would devour libraries. And I began to do something, which has followed me to this day. I would visit used bookstores. See, I've got first editions of most of the major works. But I got my first editions for twenty-five cents, thirty cents, a dollar, two dollars. Books became my life. My personal library is around 35,000 titles right now. And I've given away part of it. I gave a thousand books to Chicago State last year. So every place I would go, every place I would travel, every place I was stationed or visited, I would visit used bookstores.

Luckily I was stationed in the Chicago area. I was stationed at Arlington Heights, Missile Barracks. Then I was stationed at Fort Sheridan for a while. As a result of that, I came to the DuSable Museum and I hooked up with Margaret Burroughs and Charlie Burroughs. Now, the interesting thing about this is that both Margaret and Charlie are pretty left wing. They're real left. I mean Charlie Burroughs was raised in Russia, the USSR. And Charlie introduced me to the Russian writers like Chekov. The major Russian writers I got through Charlie Burroughs. They both had one of the best libraries that I knew of at that time.

Margaret and Charlie kind of adopted me, and I helped build the early phase of the museum. I was a volunteer for about three years, from 1962 to 66. And anytime a Russian delegation would go through Chicago, they'd always hit the museum. So I would meet them. Margaret and Charlie were always very political, very political. So I was able to see how they functioned. And they were my early influence on the importance of institutions because, see, the DuSable Museum was first in their home. They lived on Thirty-eighth and Michigan Avenue. The first floor was the museum, and eventually the basement was the museum and they lived on the second floor. That's where their library was and so forth. And I became somewhat of an assistant curator, which was basically just showing people through the museum and talking about Black history and stuff like that. It was actually Margaret Burroughs who really suggested that I publish my book. That's how I began to get the poetry out there.

Lita: You're back, out of the Army. You're in Chicago. The Civil Rights Movement's gaining momentum. What memories do you have of organizations, members here in Chicago?

Haki: Well, I came out of the military in August 1963, and in September of '63 four little Black girls were murdered in Birmingham, Alabama, and the question for me was a very serious question. What do you do? I mean, here, we're still in apartheid USA. You got these crazy people killing our children. I'd been taught to be a killer the last three years. What do you do? Do you join the killers of the world, or do you try to do something in terms of working with your people? That was part of the dilemma. It was not a great dilemma, because I had pretty much made that decision in terms of the literature and the problems I went through in the military. I was almost killed in the military because of this whole racial thing. And so when I came out, I got an apartment on Sixty-third and Ada. I lived in a basement apartment on Sixty-third and Ada and continued to work with the museum and went to school. I went to, at that time it was Wilson Junior College, it's Kennedy-King now. We're talking about 1963. I worked nights. I worked at the stockyards, you know, wherever I could pick up work. I worked at the Post Office for a couple of years at night and did a small amount of work at Spiegels as a Junior Executive in the early 60s.

I began to work with CORE primarily, the Congress of Racial Equality, here in Chicago. Robert Lucas, Bob Lucas at that time was the chair of CORE. But my major work was trying to write and publish. I eventually met two men who would basically direct me and showed some interest in my work. That was Dudley Randall, who became my first publisher. He was the publisher at Broadside Press. And Hoyt W. Fuller, who was the managing editor of *Negro Digest* (*Black World*) magazine. But prior to my meeting Dudley Randall, I'd published my own book, my first book. It was *Think Black*. I published that in 1966, myself. I threw the poems together. In fact, there was another man, a man by the name of Eugene Feldman. He was a white Jewish man who worked with Margaret Burroughs and Charlie Burroughs and was committed to Black folks. He would be one of these men...I'd just say he was a good man. And he suggested actually the cover for the book. I'd come up with the title, *Think Black*. Eugene said, "Why don't you put Africa on the book?" So I got a picture of Africa and put it on there and took these poems to a Black printer on the west side of Chicago. I had searched around to get the best price and I could do 600 copies for 200 to 300 dollars.

So I got it done and that started me as a published poet and as a publisher, too. So I'm understanding the process. Now what do you do with 600 books and you don't have a distributing network? So in 1966 I got these books, I began working a little bit with SNCC and eventually ended up working with SCLC, when Jesse Jackson came to town and stuff like that. I'd sell the books at the rallies. I'd stand at Sixty-third and Cottage Grove under the el and sell the books. Whenever King would come, at the rallies, you know I was at most of the marches in Chicago. However, my major involvement was with OBAC, Organization of Black American Culture Writer's Workshop.

I was one of the founding members of the Writer's Workshop. Hoyt Fuller and I had become like big brother, younger brother and he saw something of value in my work and began to publish my work regularly in *Negro Digest*. I broke into *Negro Digest* primarily as a book reviewer. I would review a lot of books, and eventually as a poet. So that was just a very, very important relationship.

So we're still talking around 1966 to 1967, and then I think in the summer of 1967 I met Gwendolyn Brooks. Gwendolyn Brooks was teaching a writer's workshop to a segment of the Blackstone Rangers at a church right here on the south side of Chicago. Oscar Brown Jr. was putting on this big production and Gwendolyn was out there teaching. So I, and some of the poets, went down there just to check her out. And from that point on, we just continued to go, and eventually that workshop moved into her home and became the Gwendolyn Brooks Workshop. At the same time Gwendolyn Brooks moved from Harper and Row to Broadside Press. And by then Broadside Press had published my next book, which was *Black Pride*. Dudley Randall wrote the introduction for it.

Around 1967 or 1968, under J. Edgar Hoover's leadership the FBI initiated COINTELPRO, which was a counter-intelligence program to disrupt the Black movement. He had targeted mainly the major civil rights organizations: SCLC, NAACP, CORE. They did not know too much about the underground movement until the Panthers hit, and they got targeted, as well as other groups.

You had the Red Squad here in Chicago. And you had a certain amount of fear element coming in because every time you turned around, you didn't know whether you were dealing with the FBI, undercover cops or what the case was. So the whole struggle took on another whole life of its own.

So in 1969 I went to Algiers (Algeria) for the first time for a festival. Gwendolyn Brooks was very instrumental in helping me go there. In fact, she encouraged me to go. We had heard about this big festival, and at that time a lot of the Panthers had left the country and were living in Algiers. This is where the third world struggle was happening. Of course, Frantz Fanon writes lovingly about Algiers. I wanted to go there just to see the square that was named after Frantz Fanon. Anyway, I went, which was my first trip to Africa. I went by myself. It was a very important trip because, again, it was the first time I was ever out of the country, other than to Mexico and Canada. But

I'd never gone across the ocean anywhere. So I got to Algiers and that is where I met Nina Simone, Archie Shepp and Ted Joans, the poet. Okay, by 1968, I had published two books. *Think Black!* and *Black Pride*. Yeah, Broadside Press published *Black Pride* and Dudley Randall wrote the introduction to it. In the first part of the year in 1968, I was invited to Fisk University for a writers' conference sponsored every year by Fisk University, under the direction of John Oliver Killens. Now, obviously I wanted to go to this, and then he invited me to be a presenter. I was very excited because John Killens' work had influenced me a great deal. I had read all of his novels and had read his book of essays.

So I came, and by that time my work was being celebrated in certain quarters, and when I got down there, several things happened. When I got down there I met Robert Hayden, the great poet. Robert Hayden was teaching at Fisk University, but he and John Killens were poles apart in terms of the politics. Hayden did not consider himself a Black writer; he just saw himself as a writer. Even though, if you read his poetry, it is some of the best poetry in the universe written about Black folks.

I saw Robert Hayden going across the quad, you know, across the green. And I called out to him and he stopped and I introduced myself. He invited me to his home, and we sat down and had tea. We talked and he listened to me and basically told me where I was wrong. He did it in a way that was not too negative. But it didn't sit with me too well, so I left and went back to the conference and that's where I met Nikki. Nikki Giovanni. She was finishing her last year down there at Fisk University. And we became friends.

I gave a reading there and the place just erupted. As a result of that reading and my poetry at the whole conference, I was offered two jobs. I was offered a job at Talledega College in Alabama, and I was offered a job at Cornell University up in Ithaca, New York.

When I came back here to Chicago, I talked to Gwen about it, and Hoyt, and George Kent. These were the kind of people I listened to. George Kent was the great critic; one of the first Blacks to receive a tenured professorship at the University of Chicago. He did a book on Gwendolyn Brooks. So I said, "I want to go to Talledega. I want to go to a Black school." And they said, "Why don't you go on down there first and take the opportunity to speak down there? Don't close the door on Cornell."

So I took their advice and went down to Talledega. It was a nice campus. Nice and warm and everything. Probably if I'd gotten that job, my life would've changed. It probably would have been a lot different. Once I spoke, they wouldn't give me the job. They didn't want that kind of fire, that kind of political mind on that campus. Now, I'm talking late 60s.

So I didn't get that job and decided to go on up to Cornell. But the Cornell job was not a given either. They didn't want me to speak. They brought me into the English department and had these five men, these white elderly men in the English department. They were sitting around this table, it was about four of them, four men, I made five. What they were doing was seeing if I was qualified to teach at Cornell. They were grilling me on Black literature. But I discovered very early that only one of the men there, I don't remember his name, knew anything about Black literature. The others probably read *Invisible Man* and *Native Son*. That was it. So I basically turned the interview around and questioned them about the literature. I got the job. It was 1969. I'd have to go back and look at my notes, but I'm pretty sure I went to Africa prior to going to Cornell.

I used to read poetry every place here in the city. And with OBAC and even the Gwendolyn Brooks poetry workshop, we used to go into bars and taverns and just stop stuff and just read. I remember one night I was reading at the Southerland, the new Southerland on Forty-seventh Street and Drexel Avenue, at that time they used to do jazz at least once or twice a week. I don't remember what the occasion was, but I was reading poetry there that night. I read a poem—I don't even remember the poem—but anyway, a writer from *Ebony* [Magazine] was there. His name was David Llorens. He worked for *Negro Digest/Black World*, but he was writing for *Ebony* at that time. David and I were about the same age. His life dream was to be a writer. We all had been influenced by Baldwin, influenced by Wright, influenced by all the major writers coming along at that time. I mean writing was in our blood. This was like musicians who wanted to be the next Trane or Cannonball Adderly or Lee Morgan, or whatever the case may be.

We wanted to be the next Baldwin or Gwendolyn Brooks. David and I didn't know each other, but I read the poem and the last line of the poem is:

> Jesus Saves
> Jesus Saves
> Jesus Saves
> S+H Green Stamps

And David fell off the stool, primarily because he was raised Catholic. This was like blasphemous, and he had never heard anything like this in terms of poetry. So he came up and said, "Show me these poems." I mean Black poetry, especially the type we were writing, was like, "This is just not happening." We became close, not too close, but we became acquaintances in the whole writing community. We stayed in communication and he said, "Haki, let me write a story about you for *Ebony*." And, I mean, *Ebony* is the biggest thing out there. I said, "Damn. Sure." I just had two books out but he said, "Okay, I can sell this to John Johnson, because you're at Cornell, not because of the two books, but because you're the Black writer in residence at Cornell University."

So he comes up to Cornell and they sent the major photographer up to there and they stayed with me for about three or four days. He was just going to class with me, recording everything and wrote the story. By that time I had finished most of *Don't Cry, Scream* and Dudley was getting ready to publish it. It almost coincided with the article in Ebony of March 1969. And so, *Don't Cry, Scream* just jumped. It sold easily over 250,000 copies, and that's how Don Lee became known on a national level. You had *Ebony* with the article, and then you had *Don't Cry, Scream*, and everybody was carrying this red and black book with my face on it.

Lita: Anymore defining moments?

Haki: The founding of Third World Press in 1967 in my basement apartment on the south side of Chicago. I had earned some money...maybe about three or four hundred dollars from a poetry reading or something...and had purchased this used mimeograph machine and I called Johari Amini, who was Jewell Latimore at that time, and Carolyn Rodgers. We were all students. I said, "Let's start this poetry group." Johari and Carolyn said, "Yeah, let's do it." They didn't have any money or nothing like that. But I basically wanted to include these other poets. Carolyn Rodgers came up with the name Third World Press, and we just published their first two books. We published *Songs of Blackbird*, and that was Carolyn's first book. *Images in Black* was Johari's book. But we did it on this mimeograph machine, and that started Third World Press. Carolyn Rodgers only stayed with us about two or three months, and then she went to a major white press. But off and on, Johari stayed with us for about ten years, until she decided to go into medicine. She's a chiropractor now.

So Third World Press was kind of a labor of love. We started in my basement apartment, then we moved to Ellis Bookstore on Sixty-third and Cottage Grove. Then once I got back from Cornell we got the place, two storefronts on 78th and Ellis. It's right across the street from our school. On the corner. So we got those two storefronts. One storefront was for the press, Third World Press, and the other storefront was for the Institute of Positive Education.

I'd always felt that the publishing company is important, fine. But I've got this activist spirit, so the books and another spirit are saying we got to deal with these children and we started the Institute of Positive Education. And we basically dealt with children in this community. After school tutoring, all day Saturday, African-centered programs. We used to run past this place all the time. We used to exercise right across in the park. We used to run everyday just to stay in shape. We used to run past the school and say what could we do if we had a school like this someday.

Lita: The 60s were a very busy time for you.

Haki: That was the 60s. The 60s were very heady days. I think what closed the 60s for me, metaphorically, was the murder of Fred Hampton and Mark Clark. There are some other things that went down, too. Obviously the rebellions, as a result of the murder of King, and obviously it was another awakening when Malcolm was murdered in 1965. It was another whole awakening. But even though I had met King, I never met Malcolm. I did not know King. I was not a confidante. I just met him. I was a foot soldier at that time. But Fred and I were almost the same age and we would just talk. I did not know Mark Clark. But when they murdered Fred right here in Chicago that was just frightening. Of course, I had some military background and I just went and bought some more weapons, because I felt like, at this point, this must be it. And I was going to go do something because he was basically killed by some Black cops. But I was talked out of that by some people.

As a result of that whole thing with Fred Hampton and Mark Clark, I went back to Africa for some reason. Anyway it was after that Africa trip that I wrote *We Walk the Way of the New World*. I felt that our struggle had been demoralized.

You had COINTELPRO, you had the Red Squad in Chicago and you had local police receiving all this money from the federal government, basically to disrupt the Black movement. And so I saw brothers and sisters turning to anti-social behavior, drugs, alcohol. And having come out of a dysfunctional family, I knew that wasn't the answer. I'm probably one of the few persons in the struggle, the Black struggle period, who has never been high. I never drank anything. I never smoked. I've never been involved in trying to diminish one's own life by such anti-social behavior. At the same time, I was always looking, trying to find out, what is the answer? What is the answer? In 1970, I was offered a position at Howard University. I accepted and went to teach there in the Institute of the Arts and Humanities.

Obviously, I came through the church and had very negative experiences in the church. We'd started the Congress of African People. Karenga had been put in captivity because of some problems out there on the West Coast. We were dealing in the early days with this whole question of Kawaida. So for about four years we were involved with the Congress of African People. We were also involved with the African Liberation Support Committee. We were all African-centered at that point. We're trying to move toward some closure on apartheid in South Africa and most importantly the type of colonialism and neocolonialism that still existed in much of Africa. We're working diligently in our own way trying to deal with these problems, all these problems. So I'm saying, you look at all this coming on. We're trying to deal with education here in Chicago. Trying to deal with the publishing company. I'm traveling back and forth to Howard every week, as well as doing readings and trying to raise money because for everything…there has never been any grants and stuff. All my money has gone into building these institutions. All of it. Every penny.

At the same time, we began to have some difficulty with Mr. Johnson of Johnson Publishing, Co. Now, I, along with some other artists set up picket lines around John Johnson's *Ebony*, *Jet*, and *Negro Digest* building, because we were just totally upset with this man continuing to advertise these skin whiteners and all this negative, middle–class, Black stuff that we felt had nothing to do with the majority of the Black community. And he was not supporting Black struggle in print at the level we felt most effective. So we set up a picket line outside the old office building. This was before they moved into the new place on Michigan Avenue. Mr. Johnson met with us and said he was going to pull those ads out and he gave some money to a couple of theater groups. And we went on home.

About a year or two years later we became upset. At that first picket line we demanded that he change the name from *Negro Digest* to *Black World Magazine*. So that's how that happened. That was the first time that I publicly went on a picket line against John Johnson. So we're moving on into the 1970s.

Now, Hoyt Fuller, as far as I'm concerned, was one of the main architects of this whole Black Arts Movement. Because through the pages of *Negro Digest/Black World Magazine*, you had the theoretical basis being built. You had the theory being built. I was writing essays. [Amiri] Baraka was writing essays. Harold Cruse was writing essays. You got John Oliver Killens writing essays. You got John H. Clarke. You got Addison Gayle Jr. writing essays. You got some of the best minds in our struggle really bringing forth the theory of Black struggle, most certainly Black literary struggle through the pages of *Black World*. And Hoyt Fuller was the catalyst for all of that.

I became aware of Diop's work through [this] struggle and began to publish Baraka and Diop eventually. So we had, we felt, at one level, a kind of a prize here. We had one of the major poets and one of the major minds, if not the major magazine editor, Black magazine editor, most certainly, in the world. There was no other magazine that had the reach of *Negro Digest/Black World*. It had a minimum publication of over 50,000 each month. And for *Negro Digest/Black World* you multiply that by ten readers per issue. It was just that valuable. We'd just go through that magazine from front to back. Each issue was just like a rallying call. It would just lay out what was happening.

Lita: Oh, my goodness. I'm all confused now. I'm going to go back to the 60s and the Black Arts Movement. Did you feel like you were a part of a national movement with goals and a sense of direction? Will you talk about the founding of OBAC and who was part of it and your goals for OBAC?

Haki: Well, we always felt we were much larger than we were because we knew that there were strong pockets in New York, Los Angeles, San Francisco. There was this whole feeling of empowerment. We had the music; we had the visual arts; we had the poetry; we had fiction. They had this whole gigantic movement, which we were all a part of. And which, basically, kept us narrow and straight, because this movement was like surrogate mothers and fathers. And most certainly during the later part of the 60s you had these Black power conferences going on. You'd go to these conferences and you just said, "Yeah, we can do this." It was like at one point, you forgot because this deep brotherhood and sisterhood would drag us around the world and most certainly around the country. But we were not just writers, because you had the musicians and you had the visual artists and you had other people doing the same thing.

I mean here in Chicago, we put up one of the first murals, The Wall of Respect, right there on Forty-third for those that got international publicity. Then, of course, with Ms. Brooks leaving Harper and Row and going with Broadside Press, we didn't think we could do anything wrong. Here we were building our own institutions. It was very exciting. Very heavy.

But yes, to answer your question. We felt that we were part of a strong national movement. And OBAC, we felt, was the center of it. We're getting ready to publish a book by Kalaamu Ya Salaam, *The Magic of JuJu*, which is on the history of the Black Arts Movement.

But there were several pockets of this whole Black Arts Movement developing, and Chicago was like the center. Chicago was almost like the communications center. You had Johnson here; you had Third World Press coming here. You had the Midwest; you had Detroit with Broadside Press. So Chicago was pivotal. Obviously you had Gwendolyn Brooks; Hoyt Fuller was here, you had Lerone Bennett, in terms of one of the major historians. Like I mentioned, George Kent was here. Then you had other writers and poets here in Chicago.

Then you had the New York center. You know, centered around Baraka, the Lafayette Theater, Ed Bullins and people like that. Then on the West Coast you had, especially out in the Bay Area, you had Sonia Sanchez out there and Eldridge Cleaver coming up through the Panthers out there. *The Journal of Black Poetry* was one of the major vehicles.

Hoyt Fuller was like a big brother to me. I'm saying he loaned me five or six hundred dollars to buy a car so that I could go to Ithaca, New York, to teach at Cornell and I'm sure all the other writers were hitting on him, too. He was the reason that OBAC flourished, and lived, really until he left. The reason he left was because John Johnson fired him. And he fired him because Hoyt would not stop publishing both sides of the Israel–Palestinian conflict. I'm saying the man had integrity. He was basically publishing both sides of the Israeli–Palestinian problem. Whereas in this country, as in much of the western world, the Israeli narrative is predominate, and the Palestinian narrative is almost unheard.

Lita: There are three areas I want to discuss. One was that you have remained an activist. You have also remained, well, as an artist you continued to develop. I want to talk about the evolution in your work and how you go from poetry to essays and why. And the other thing is that you remained rooted in the community. Can you talk a little about that? How were you able to do those three things?

Haki: Well, the activism came about as a result of my early life. I just felt that one cannot achieve without doing. So the activism is just an extension of politics. Which means essentially that I had, unlike many of the young activists of that time, read a tremendous amount of Black literature, even [compared to] those folks I was working with in CORE, that I worked with even in OBAC, that I was working with in SCLC or SNCC. In many cases these young people were not as well read as I was. Therefore, the literature had informed my life on a different level. So the activism was like the blood in the veins. I've always felt that to get anything done, you had to be active. One of the reasons we started the Institute of Positive Education was because I felt that the publishing company was just not an activist entity enough for me.

The poetry, the whole artist side...I was tremendously influenced by Langston Hughes and Gwendolyn Brooks. What I saw in Gwendolyn Brooks was the real artist at work, which means essentially that she gave her time and knowledge to young poets and most of her money away. She worked and functioned in the community. Gwen used to live basically from here about ten blocks. But from our old location she just lived around the corner. You could ask Gwendolyn Brooks for anything, and if she had it she would give it to you. There weren't any questions. What I learned from Gwendolyn Brooks was her religion of...what she would call her religion of kindness. And that she felt that if one is kind, if there is any justice in the universe, than it's going to come back. She never said that she was going to retire. She felt that she was always going to write. And if she could write, she could always make a living.

Black people have short memories. So if you're not publishing every year, at least then, you're going to be forgotten. So with the poetry...the poetry kept coming. *Think Black: Black Pride, Don't Cry, Scream, We Walk The Way Of The New World*. In 1971 I published two books, a selected poems collection, *Directionscore*, and a book of criticism, *Dynamite Voice: Black Poets of the 1960s*. Now, you get to 1973, 'cause what's happening is you've got The Congress of African People. I'm writing these essays, but I'm not publishing them in book form. They're being published in magazines. In 1973, two books come out, *From Plan to Planet* and *Book of Life*. Now at the same time I'm making another choice. I'm changing my name. *From Plan to Planet* comes first, and then with *Book of Life* there's a name change happening.

The essays were basically political and cultural essays as a result of all this work. In some sense they're theoretical pieces, but in another sense they're not theory because they are what we've been trying to do for the last four or five years. But I realized too that there is a whole segment of Black people out here who do not read poetry, may not even get to the poetry, but would pick up a book of essays. So I'm thinking too, especially since I'm also teaching at Howard. So I'm getting another view of the Black intelligentsia at Howard. They will read certain things. Most will not read poetry. There's this kind of alienation from the poetry. But the essays gave me another life as a writer.

I was saying, we had gone through all this pain, all this disruption and all this murder in our community. Our community had been flooded with drugs, businesses pulled out, so *Book of Life*, for me, was saying, "How do we hold on? How do we keep going?" So that whole poetry was very much a part of what I felt was an answer. But at the same time, I knew that there had to be more, quote unquote, concrete directives. And that's how, *Plan to Planet* came about.

Now, after *Plan to Planet*, came *Enemies*. *Enemies* was the first book of essays after *Plan to Planet* but basically geared toward the whole struggle of the 70s. By that time I'd gone to 6th PAC. I'd gone to FESPAC. 6th PAC was in Tanzania. FESPAC was in Nigeria. I'd gone to the first conference in Senegal—this conference dealing with Black intellectuals. That's where Harold Cruse and I became close, in Senegal. So I'm saying that's at least three trips to Africa in the 70s. I'm trying to think if there were more. There might have been one or two others. But that African consciousness had just clung. It had attached itself, so my name was changed in 1974 from Don Lee to Haki R. Madhubuti.

So it's this whole...it's a very deep, deep commitment. For me the artist part was not in conflict with activist part. Nor was it in conflict with the theoretical part, in terms of saying that at some point you're going to try to write some theory or these other people are going to write it. Now, see, during this period we had these real battles, this ongoing battle with the left. There was a whole segment of the Black left trying to make us into the Black left and trying to get us to work with the White left. We had a whole segment of the Black revolutionary community, mainly the Panther Party, trying to get us to work with the White left.

I went to a number of these secret meetings, not a lot, but several secret meetings in New York and other places meeting with these people. But I could just see that this was very detached from the Black community. They got this rhetoric out here. They got this Marxist-Leninist, Mao Tse-Tung theory out here, but had no attachment to our community. It's alien. I didn't come out of a Black middle class, privileged family where the children attended Howard or Fisk or any-place else. I came out of the central core of the Black community and stayed there all my life. So I knew, and had read a lot, of the left stuff early. These people had not even read Richard Wright or Robeson. They went straight to the White left. So Baraka jumps up here in 1974, and says, "I'm a Marxist-Leninist" and his actions caused the dismantling of the Congress of African People. See, our chapter of the Congress of African People sponsored the Midwest meeting of the Congress of African People and he got up there and said, "I'm a Communist now." At that point, that was it. We split. That's when he came out with both feet jumping on Haki Madhubuti. Basically talking about nothing that had to do with politics. He talked about my diet. It didn't have nothing to do with politics. And so we split up. By that time we had published two, three of his books. We had published, *It's Nation Time*, *Jello*, and *Kawaida Studies*. And maybe one other. And so we just split at that point.

It was just a very negative period in my life. Here we were going on with a Nationalist Pan-Africanist program. It was never, we felt, anything other than trying to rebuild these communities. See, one thing that I've always been aware of is the economic question. I knew we didn't have any money. If we're talking about real resources, we don't have any real money. I'm not confused about that. Now here comes the question: now, you know that you've got the Kennedy's; you've got the Rockefellers; you've got the Buckley's—what they walk around with as spending money, just chump change, is more than we got. So the question at one point is, do you write grants to these peo-

ple? Or do you take what you have? What any people who are in control of their own cultural imperatives, this is what Harold Cruse taught
us, you say, "Okay, you take what you have and start dealing with that."
What I did know, coming from the Lumpenproletariat, was that you
cannot depend upon people who don't like you. We have not even got
to the point of racism. They just don't like us. These same people who
don't like you will be smiling in your face all day long, talking about
how good a writer you are, when they go out to the committee and get
your application for the grant they say, no. So why give them the opportunity to do that? Why give them the pleasure of turning you down?
You can use the same energy to build something in your own community.

But everyday you've got to make this commitment. It is not a
sacrifice. Don't confuse it. I think when people become adults, when
people understand what the world requires of us, that we make a commitment to the world, to ourselves, everyday a commitment. And just
because I haven't eaten well sometimes, or just because I don't have a
new car every year, just because I don't have a whole lot of clothes that
everybody else has, just because I don't have the kind of house that I
really want. I haven't sacrificed. I've made a commitment to this type
of struggle.

Lita: What about your contemporaries? Why do you think that some
people who came out of the Movement didn't maintain that sense of
commitment? I mean this is what it was all about and yet, mid–70s you
see people go in different directions.

Haki: Well, I think the COINTELPRO issue had a real big effect. It
scared a lot of people. When the federal government says the Black
struggle is over, they fail to understand COINTELPRO's involvement
in the undercover disruption of the Black Movement. I mean, they
came down on us like a ton of bricks. Your files were pulled; everybody
was identified in files and everything. Go to the Freedom of Informa-
tion Act and see if you can get my file. That happened and that was
scary. When Mark Clark and Fred Hampton were killed here in
Chicago, it scared a lot of people. At the same time you had these mur-

ders all over the country that we didn't even know about. You had these local areas and you had brothers disappearing.

Then you had a lot of problems in the 70s going into the 80s. This drug thing hit, and a lot of people in the struggle got hooked on drugs. And once you get into that mess, you're gone. You're not any good to anybody.

In terms of a lot of the artists, writers, many of them made their own choices and these choices were not necessarily bad for them. Even though Baraka and I had our disagreements, I've always felt Baraka was committed to Black folks. We just didn't agree for a good period of time. But when you look at the writers who have been very inspirational to me—Sonia Sanchez never did sway. Mari Evans didn't sway. Gwendolyn Brooks most certainly didn't sway. Ishmael Reed is very serious. And if you look at writers who were not necessarily a part of this whole Black Arts Movement, but were effected by it, the John Edgar Widemans, the Walter Mosleys. That's that generation that came after us. But I think we affected them in a very powerful way. Some people were never able to kind of break that threshold where you get a national hearing. Askia Toure, I think at one level, he's a fine writer, been around a long time, but he was not able to like, break it. You know, he's one of the architects of the Black Arts Movement. I think that's what probably gave me that national push was that *Ebony* magazine article. 'Cause when *Don't Cry, Scream* took off and Gwendolyn Brooks wrote the introduction, it sold about half a million copies.

At that time, this is 1969, if I sold a half million now, it would translate into 3 to 4 million in terms of what some of the sisters and brothers are doing today. I think for me, being in Chicago, being around Hoyt Fuller, and Gwendolyn Brooks and Margaret and Charlie Burroughs, being so close to Detroit and Dudley Randall, and brothers and sisters that I knew up in Detroit was helpful to staying committed to the struggle.

And then some of the brothers and sisters went into religion. They got captured by the church. That might have been very positive for them, and I'm sure that it was, but for me, I just felt that this was my life. And still feel that way. This will be my life. I don't see any retirement.

I'm one of the few writers fortunate enough to be able to build a life out of this work. I've never taken any money from Third World Press, from our schools or from the bookstores. So I've never been on salary. I've never been on salary, primarily because I never wanted anybody to say, "Haki's doing this so he could make money." You have that kind of smallness out here. So I've always taught or worked outside.

Lita: You say you taught at Iowa. I was at Iowa for a year, with Dr. Darwin Turner, the year he died actually. I was his graduate assistant. We talked about you. Didn't you attend the Iowa Writer's Workshop?

Haki: I did. George Kent and Darwin T. Turner were critical in trying to develop a Black literary theory. I met Darwin back in...probably in the early 70s. I don't remember when, because I've met a whole lot of people then. But Darwin had shown a great appreciation for my work.

I left Howard and I was very tired. I'm traveling to D.C. every week; I'm reading poetry at least 30 to 40 times a year someplace; I'm traveling back and forth to Africa, if not Africa then to other places in the world. I'm just tired. In fact, I was tired in 1977, but I asked the vice president [of Howard], I said, "Look every place I've been, I've published at least one book. But I haven't published one book since I've been at Howard." Both *From Plan to Planet* and *Book of Life* were written prior to my going to Howard. So I said, "Let me finish this last book. Let me give it one more year and just write this book." That was the 1977-1978 academic year. I think I just taught one course and wrote *Enemies: The Clash of Races*. And I also helped people get jobs here in Chicago. I wrote letters for them and I knew many of the people here in higher education.

So I called Darwin. This had to be in the 80s 'cause I was there in 1982. Now what I did in between there, I started commuting again. I taught at Central State in Ohio. I did that for about a year. And I'd do these short residencies at colleges and universities. Then it got to a point where people said, "We can't give you a job with any kind of benefits unless you have a terminal degree." So, I'm saying, "Where can I get a terminal degree?" I know I'm not going to work on a Ph.D. I'm just not going to do that. I'd published at that point about twelve books. So I called Darwin and I said, "Darwin, what do you think about my getting into the MFA program at the Writers Workshop?" At that time I'd had about twelve books and twelve years of teaching and publishing. Darwin had some reservations because of the conservatism of the university.

So he invited me down to speak. They wanted to hear what I had to say. I knew I was being tested, so I just basically lectured on Black literature. I got into the program. I didn't have an undergrad degree. I just had that Associate's Degree and a few hours at a senior college. Darwin said, "I want you to teach in my program here." So I taught a couple of courses in his program, and I went into the MFA studies in the Iowa Writer's Workshop.

But Darwin was very helpful, because he gave me a job. I left in '84. Darwin asked me to stay one additional semester, because he'd lost somebody. I'm driving up there every week. Who's going to live in Iowa? So I'm driving up there every week and Darwin said, "I just need some help. Will you stay one more semester?" So I did. I taught a course on Saturday. I'd drive up on Friday evenings, teach Saturday and come back Saturday night. Generally, I'd do the Tuesday through Thursday thing like I had at Howard. They were just paying me a regular salary, so I just bought a car and drove over five hundred miles a week.

That's why I'm saying; don't talk to me about education being hard or difficult. I don't want to hear it. I don't take any excuses from my students. You've got to get this work done, and I'm serious. I'm saying, whatever excuse you can come up with I've heard it already and I know all about it. Just trying to get this Masters of Fine Arts, driving for two years between Iowa City and Chicago. Because I can't leave Chicago. I can't move my family up to Iowa. I'm driving up there every week and still trying to do all this other work.

Lita: So, regarding the family life and strong marriage and being a good father, is all that, for you, part of the activism, the community, the art?

Haki: Oh, yeah. Absolutely. The love of Safisha and my family has been kind of the backbone that gives me that central strength. You see, I don't see life without children, without family. I don't buy into this lonely artist. The writer, the painter, the musician. We all need somebody. We are social beings. You try to develop a relationship that is lasting and loving and is going to mean something.

And at the same time it gets back to commitments, what do you see as important. I see that in terms of trying to build our communities. I don't see them being built without families. I just don't see that. And I think these commitments have to be made and they have to be lasting. I'm not saying they're not going to be difficult, that you are not going to have rough times. We've had rough times and we understand that relationships are not perfect, but what are you committed to? I mean, there is nothing more important to me than my family. I'm saying at one point that even if we'd built these institutions and I didn't have a family, then it seems that there is a certain amount of failure. Because in the final and most important analysis, working and loving families represent the substance of any nation. Therefore, the first struggle is to rear healthy, intelligent, and loving children with a work ethic and knowledge-seeking ethic that works toward making the world a better place for all of its inhabitants. This requires mature-minded and serious families who represent the first teachers and examples for children.

I think the key point is that activism and conflict are natural byproducts of political and cultural struggle. If you've got conflict at home in terms of struggle, and you and your mate are not communicating, it's not going to last. I've seen it happen too many times. So Safisha and I both have been involved in this awesome struggle all of our adult lives. It has worked for us.

Lita: She was involved with both the founding of the Institute, as well as the school?

Haki: New Concept School? Yes, all of our schools; in fact, she is the guiding spirit and chairperson of our board. I had founded the press prior to my meeting her. She was involved in the press in the early days, but not too much. Her major responsibility was basically with the school.

Lita: I wanted to ask you about major influences. You talked about Gwendolyn Brooks. Is there anything you want to add?

Haki: Well, I'd say Gwendolyn Brooks is probably the major influence and the most sustaining and the longest. Gwendolyn Brooks and I are like mother and son. She's like a cultural mother. She has been for over thirty-three years. Her example and her support, her cultural and emotional support, and her financial support have been the key in terms of my development. And her coming to Third World Press was very important to the life of the press. It was in the early 70s when she gave us two books. She gave us *The Tiger Who Wore White Gloves*, a children's book. Then she came back and we published a poetry book and now we are her primary publisher. We published *Report From Part Two*, which is the second part of her autobiography. In 2003, we posthumously published her book *In Montgomery*.

Lita: In terms of your own work, I've always wondered why you never ventured into fiction and drama.

Haki: Oh, I have fiction.

Lita: You do?

Haki: I have a novel. Two novels. I just haven't published them.

Lita: Really?

Haki: I have a novel, one I have titled, *Eight Weeks Plus Death*. It deals with my basic training and the time some White men tried to kill me in the Army. And then, I've been working off-and-on on this book, it's kind of a piece of fiction but it's kind of a love novel.

Drama is another genre that I'm just not comfortable with. I support the theater here to a great extent, but I just never really ventured into that area. I feel that if I can do good work in poetry and good work in the essays, and then struggle with my fiction, that'll be okay, Probably within the next three years I'll get the fiction out. I'll feel a little more comfortable with it.

The key point in all of this is that, writers like myself and Gwendolyn Brooks and Baraka, and others who are activists, we don't get writer's block. We never don't have something to write about. Just college professors get writer's block. If you have to deal with survival everyday, you always have something to write about.

Lita: In terms of your early poetry do you see any clear evolution in your work? I mean, where you were then, where you are now?

Haki: Oh, absolutely.

Lita: Can the critics put your work in categories? I've found it very hard to do.

Haki: I don't know if I can categorize any of the books. I think that basically, ideologically, they are all going along the same path. I think that in terms of skill, craft and writing…obviously you don't just stand still, you develop. I think you can look at *GroundWork* and see that all the way through. I think that's good. Maturation is there. Subject matter has pretty much been the same. The Black community will always be my subject. I'm not interested in writing about white people or anybody else. I don't know enough about them, other than what I've observed living with them. I don't think I can go sub–surface with white folks. I choose to basically function and work in this community. *HeartLove* (1998) and *Tough Notes* (2002) are different books but carry the same message, the love of Black people and the continued need for development.

It has never not been a struggle. Other people, say, look at my books and they think that I've made a lot of money off of them. It's not like I haven't been coveted by white publishers. Random House came after me; University of Illinois came after me. But I said, "I'm staying here." So I'm saying at one point, I cannot only look at my books. I can look at all the other books that Third World Press has published. I can look at these structures, these institutions that are ours. So nobody tells me what to do, or not do; what to publish, or not publish. The same in the schools. Nobody tells us what to teach, or not teach. So I'm saying, I'm probably one of the freest Black men alive—

in the world. And I realize this. I'm political enough to realize that what we do here, we can't do in Nigeria. We can't do in Rwanda. We can't do, probably, in South Africa. The measure of the seriousness of any people, you look at their institutions. In the final analysis, that's what it is.

So, yes, I could write the books, and work like that, and I put a lot of time and energy into these books. But I still feel that my best work is in front of me. I really feel that. I think the next books will be on another level. Primarily built upon this experience. The future of Third World Press is just starting. I'm serious about that; we're still in our infancy after forty years. When you look at this next thirty years, then you're going to see something. Right here in the Black community, on the south side of Chicago. We could have gone downtown in the loop and rented a floor. But my decision was that, this is our community, we're not leaving this place. We can build something right here in this community that people can be proud of. And that's it.

It takes daring. It takes some insight. And this is where the reading and the studying have come in. Where all the traveling has come in. You take all of that and it comes down to this. You tap dance to the tunes that other people make, who don't even like you, or you begin to try to create your own music.

Lita: What about your perception or opinion of what's going on now, in terms of Black literature and the future? Especially in regards to young writers. I'm sure you get a lot of manuscripts.

Haki: Manuscripts all over the place. I think that there is a wealth of talent out there now that exists now that did not exist fifteen years ago. When we came along there were only about eight or nine Black bookstores in the country. At the most, only five Black publishers, and probably three of those publishers were only publishing one or two works. Now there are about twenty-five Black publishers. We have a national association, which is the National Association of Black Book Publishers. Paul Coates of Black Classic Press is the president. There are about 500 Black booksellers across the country; and out of that, maybe seventy-five bookstores. They sell out of their car, out of their homes, by mail order and other creative ways. There has been a large shift and development in terms of this whole field. The Internet has played a key role in Black book sales. Our website, www.thirdworldpressinc.com, has helped a great deal.

Young writers now have much more to choose from. And I do not demand or maintain that they have to come with us. We're here for them; we publish a lot of young writers. And we try to nurture them. But I don't have these binding contracts. You know, you publish with me first, and we have to publish your next book. I just don't believe in that. Either you want to stay with us, or you don't. That's what Dudley Randall did with me, and that's the way I operate.

I think that there is quality work out here. But some of these writers are being pushed too fast for their own good, especially a lot of the younger writers. But they have different vehicles to publish in. They have *The Source*. They have *Vibe* and they have their own magazines. And then you have these medium-sized and large publishing companies. They may touch each other at their conferences, but at the same time there is not the sense of brotherhood and sisterhood in terms of working in cultural and political struggle. And I see, at some point, opportunism. I see some of the writers getting an awful lot of money for doing very little, and they're not doing anything cultural with their money.

You've got this whole merger of hip-hop and rap and then the other level of literary literature. I mean what would have happened to Tupac, who was obviously a brilliant young man. I don't know that much about Biggie Smalls, but I had read Tupac's work and I'd heard his stuff, I saw promise there. But I saw a lot of confusion. One of the reasons he's dead is because he didn't have a responsible father. That again is why I feel that family is so critical. I write about this at some length in *Black Men* and *Tough Notes*. Women and the sisters can talk about it all they want, that they don't need the men, but the men have to be needed someplace if you're going to control these young men out here. You've got over a million Black and brown men locked up in prisons today. These are our young men. That's because in most cases their fathers are not around. There is a whole sociological cultural question we can look at long term, short term.

I know some of these young writers; I've heard and read many of these writers. I was able to find surrogate fathers, a Dudley Randall, a Hoyt Fuller. And all that is required was my going to them with some of my pain, but most certainly with talent and saying, I just need some help. I would personally never turn any person down who came to me for help or advice. It's just part of my responsibility. I'm saying there are men like me all over the country. Then, sometimes a writer arrives at a certain level and is like, "Who are you telling me what to do when I've got this?" You really can't talk to them. There is a certain naiveté.

So to answer your question, yes, you have writers at every level. But a lot of young writers out here have not read anybody. They are really literally ignorant. They really are. They could not look at the works of Sterling Brown, or Claude McKay, Margaret Danner or Margaret Walker Alexander or even Alice Walker and Toni Morrison. Most certainly Hayden, Tolson, and Toomer. I can go on down the list of Black writers that precede them.

I'm saying they only have one or two books in them, and you look at their one or two books and it's basically autobiography posing as fiction. Or I'm against this or against that. But in terms of trying to define anything or write about the beauty in the world, they're going to have difficulty, because they haven't found the beauty in our lives.

Lita: One last question: in terms of the Black Arts Movement, we talked about your involvement, but I want to know what you thought of the Movement in terms of its successes and failures?

Haki: I know that the Black Arts Movement was a great success. Obviously we all look at it from different points of view, but I think that we wouldn't exist without the Black Arts Movement. Most of the writers at the white major publishers wouldn't exist without the Black Arts Movement. What the Black Arts Movement did was redefine Black. We were Negroes until the Black Arts Movement came along. We were Negroes who rejected Africa. What the Black Arts Movement did was redefine us as Black folks, redefine us as people of African ancestry and put us on the same time line. We weren't parallel, but now we're on the same line. The Black Arts Movement moved beyond the celebrity of the individual to the necessity of a people. What you have now is a whole lot of celebrity intellectuals pontificating about a raceless society but wouldn't know how to open the front door of a serious business.

Now we have all these individuals going for themselves—individualism gone wild—trying to become the person, but in BAM we subordinated all of that. I could not have existed without Sonia Sanchez and Baraka, or Mari Evans, and Lucille Clifton—without Larry Neal and Ed Bullins and other writers. We were all, at one point, might have been in different spaces, but Hoyt Fuller was bringing us all together with *Negro Digest/Black World*. So we were feeding off of each other's work. At least I can say that. Obviously, they'd all have their own positions. I'm saying that the Movement strengthened us because we knew that we were not alone and we knew that we were right and part of a greater whole, defined as BAM. We weren't taking a self-righteous position, but truly searching for that which would benefit the majority. We knew that this was our time and nobody was going to take it from us. And I think when you look at the key persons in theatre, music and the visual arts and the literature and the dance, when you look at those key persons, they are still functioning; they are still alive. Not only are they here physically and mentally, but they are also still producing. If you didn't have the Black Arts Movement, you wouldn't have had a Toni Morrison. You wouldn't have had many of the writers. I think that all the writers who were honest must say that that Movement was useful, whether you agree with it or not. You would not be at Random House or Doubleday—we would not be at all these major white publishers today, if not for the Black Arts Movement. And most certainly you would not have all these independent Black publishers in numbers today. You wouldn't have these independent Black schools. You wouldn't have these serious African-centered churches around here today.

This movement had a tremendous influence, not only nationally, but internationally. It definitely influenced a lot of African Liberation Movements. It influenced brothers and sisters in England, the Caribbean and all over the world. So getting back to where we started from: ideas, creative ideas run the world. What idea do you have that's going to bring any kind of change? What's your idea? Now how do you do it? It's one thing to sit down and have the ideas, but it becomes another thing to take the idea from the written page and implement it. And that is the most difficult thing to do—that was the Black Arts Movement.

Literary and Cultural Timeline

1942 - Don L. Lee, born in Little Rock, Arkansas on February 23, 1942, was the first child of Maxine Graves and James Lee. Within two years of his birth the family moves to Detroit, sister Jacklyn is born and parents are separated.

1956 - Reads *Black Boy* by Richard Wright. The book influences his thinking and has a profound effect on his later life as a writer.

1957 - Reads Wright's *White Man, Listen!* which forces the young Lee to begin to think politically and makes him aware of other Black poets and writers such as Alexander Dumas, Alexander Pushkin, Phyllis Wheatley, George Moses Horton, Frances Ellen Harper, Paul Laurence Dunbar, Monroe Trotter, W.E.B. DuBois, Booker T. Washington, James Weldon Johnson, Claude McKay, Countee Cullen, Frank Horne, Arna Bontemps, Langston Hughes, Jean Toomer, Melvin B. Tolson, Sterling A. Brown, Margaret Walker, Robert E. Hayden, Gwendolyn Brooks, Chester Hines, Ralph Ellison, Ann Petry, Frank Yerby and James Baldwin.

1959 - Lee's mother dies. Lee moves to Chicago to live with his father. The reunion is a disaster. He finishes high school.

1960 - In October he joins the United States Army and is sent to Fort Leonard Wood, Missouri for Basic Training. Lee uses time in military to read close to a book a day including Paul Robeson's *Here I Stand*, and writes a 250-word essay on many of the books he reads.

1962 - Meets Margaret and Charles Burroughs at the Ebony Museum of Negro History—later renamed the DuSable Museum of African American History.

1963 - Honorably discharged from U.S. Army. Starts classes part-time at Wilson Jr. College. Continues to volunteer at DuSable Museum, eventually becomes assistant curator of exhibits.

1964 - Starts publishing poems in college newspapers and literary journals.

1965 - Malcolm X is assassinated; he had become a major influence on the young Lee. Lee credits Malcolm X with giving him his voice. Starts submitting poems to national publications.

1966 - Self-publishes first book of poetry *Think Black*. Meets Dudley Randall, who would later publish Lee's second book of poetry through his company, Broadside Press. Graduates from Wilson Jr. College. Meets Hoyt W. Fuller and becomes founding member of Organization of Black American Culture (OBAC) Writers Workshop. Begins to work with Chicago CORE (Congress of Racial Equality – Chicago) and SCLC (Southern Christian Leadership Conference).

1967 - Founded Third World Press in basement apartment on south side of Chicago with $400 earned from three poetry readings. Asked Johari Amini and Carolyn Rodgers to join him.

Meets David Llorens, attends local Student Nonviolent Coordinating Committee (SNCC) meetings with him.

Meets Gwendolyn Brooks. Ms. Brooks would become life long mentor, teacher, friend and cultural mother until her untimely death in 2000.

Meets H. Rap Brown the new head of SNCC in Detroit at Rev. Albert B. Cleage's Shrine of the Black Madonna. Rap Brown would eventually use one of Lee's poems "America Calling" in the introduction of his book *Die Nigger Die!* published in 1969.

1968 - Third World Press publishes first two books *Songs of a Black Bird* by Carolyn Rodgers and *Images in Black* by Johari Amini. Carolyn Rodgers leaves to explore other publishing opportunities. Johari Amini remains off and on in between graduate school for about ten years. Broadside Press publishes Lee's *Black Pride*.

Begins teaching Black literature at Columbia College in Chicago and Northeastern Illinois University of Chicago. Meets Barbara Ann Sizemore at a conference at a Chicago campus of Black Studies.

Receives invitation from John O. Killens to read at his annual writers conference at Fisk University—the first national stage for Lee's work. He meets the great poets Robert Hayden and Aaron Bontemps. Meets Fisk University student and young poet Nikki Giovanni.

Gloria Joseph offers him a teaching position at Cornell University. He becomes first Black poet-in-residence at an Ivy League University.

1969 - Meets James Turner who asks Lee to remain at Cornell. Lee is unable to accept because of his commitment to build Third World Press and the newly-formed Institute of Positive Education in Chicago.

He takes a position at University of Illinois at Chicago. Takes first visit to Africa. Meets Carol D. Easton; she will become his future wife.

Publishes *Don't Cry, Scream* with an introduction by Gwendolyn Brooks; sells over 50,000 copies in less than a year and a half.

David Llorens publishes major article on his work in *Ebony* magazine. Named by *Ebony* as one of the 100 most influential Black Americans.

1970-1978 - Becomes first poet-in-residence at Howard University; commutes between Chicago and Washington D.C. for the next eight years. Works with John O. Killens and Steven Henderson to revive the annual Black Writers Conference at Howard University.

1970-1980 - Works with Amiri Baraka in the Congress of African people. TWP publishes several authors including: Chancellor Williams, Amiri Baraka, George Kent, Sterling Plumpp, Angela Jackson, Hoyt W. Fuller, Dudley Randall, Sonia Sanchez, Mari Evans, Useni Eugene Perkins. Starts *Black Books Bulletin* and *Black Pages* both published by the Institute of Positive Education. TWP/IPE secures first property at 7524/26 S. Cottage Grove in Chicago, Illinois.

Receives National Endowment of the Arts and National Endowment for the Humanities Grants. Also receives Illinois Arts Council Award.

1972 - Name is changed to Haki R. Madhubuti—Kiswahili, meaning just or justice and precise, accurate and dependable.

1972- 1973 - Serves as writer-in-residence at Morgan State University in Baltimore.

1975 - Marlene Mosher, Ph.D. publishes first full-length book of criticism on the work of Don L. Lee, *New Direction from Don L. Lee* (Exposition Press).

1978-1979 - Serves as writer-in-residence at Central State University, Wilberforce, Ohio.

1970-1980 - Involved in formation of African Liberation Day celebration. Publishes *We Walk the Way of the New World, Directionscore: New and Selected Poems, Book of Life, From Plan to Planet Life Studies: The Need for African Minds and Institutions, Enemies: The Clash of Races, Kwanzaa: A Progressive and Uplifting African American Holiday, A Capsule Course in Black Poetry Writing* (co-author) and *Dynamite Voices: Black Poetry of the 1960's.*

1984 - Received an MFA from University of Iowa Creative Writing Workshop.

1987 - Joins the faculty at Chicago State University as an Associate Professor in the English Department.

1989 - Founded the Gwendolyn Brooks Center for Creative Writing and Black Literature at Chicago State University.

1990 - Founded the Gwendolyn Brooks Writers Conference at CSU.

1991 - Published *Black Men: Obsolete, Single, Dangerous? The Afrikan Family in Transition*, Third World Press with over a million copies in print. Receives an American Book Award for editing and publishing.

1995 - Co-founded *Warpland: A Journal of Black Literature, Culture and Ideas* at CSU.

1996 - Serves as a key organizer and speaker at the Million Man March Publishes *GroundWork: New and Selected Poems of Don L. Lee/ Haki R. Madhubuti, 1966-1996; Million Man March/Day of Absence: A Commemorative Anthology: Speeches, Commentary, Photography, Poetry, Illustrations and Documents.* Co-publisher and editor along with Maulana Karenga.

Was awarded Honorary Ph.D. degrees from DePaul University, Chicago, and Soujourner Douglass College, Baltimore.

1998 - Co-founded the Betty Shabazz International Charter School. Co-founded the International Literary Hall of Fame for Writers of African Descent.

2001 - Became director and co-founder of the MFA program in creative writing at Chicago State University.

2002 - Named University Distinguished Professor at Chicago State University Publishes *Tough Notes: A Healing Call for Creating Exceptional Black Men.* Inducted into the Arkansas Black Hall of Fame along with former President Bill Clinton and others.

Received the Illinois Humanities Council's Studs Terkel Humanities Service Award.

2003 - Travels to Senegal, West Africa, to serve on the preparatory committee for the Pan African Conference on Intellectuals and Cultural Workers. Honored with Haki R. Madhubuti Day at Howard University.

2004 - Publishes *Run Toward Fear: New Poems and a Poet's Hand-book*.

2005 - Publishes *YellowBlack: The First Twenty-one Years of a Poet's Life, A Memoir.*

Co-founded the Barbara A. Sizemore Middle School and the DuSable Leadership Academy in Chicago.

2006 - Received the Literary Legacy Award from the National Black Writers Conference.

Regina Jennings publishes *Malcolm X and the Poetics of Haki Mad-hubuti* (McFarland Press).

Received his third honorary Doctorate from Spelman College, Atlanta.

2007 - Third World Press celebrates its fortieth anniversary.
Publishes *Liberation Narratives: Collected Poems 1966-2007.*
Publishes *Freedom to Self Destruct: Black Light, Hard Truths, Bright Seasons Coming; The Art and Necessity of Questioning in America Se-lected Writings 1970-2007*

Since 1966 Madhubuti has worked on his poetry and prose; and has been published or critiqued in hundreds of anthologies, magazines, journals, newspapers and critical studies.

Bibliography

Fuller, Hoyt W. "Towards a Black Aesthetic." *Negro Digest.* January 1968.

Gayle, Addison. *The Black Aesthetic.* Garden City, NY: Doubleday, 1972.

Kessler, Jascha. "Trial and Error." *Poetry 121* (February, 1973): 292-293.

Llorens, David. "Black Don Lee." *Ebony*: March 1969.

Miller, Eugene. "Some Black Thoughts on Don L. Lee's Think Black! Thunk By a Frustrated White Academic Thinker." *College English 34* (May, 1973): 1094-1102.

Miller, Jeanne-Marie A. "*A Review of We Walk the Way of the New World by Don L. Lee.*" The Journal of Negro History (April, 1971):153-55.

Mosher, Marlene. *New Directions from Don L. Lee.* Hicksville, NY: Exposition, 1975.

Palmer, R. Roderick. "The Poetry of Three Revolutionists: Don L. Lee, Sonia Sanchez, and Nikki Giovanni." *College Language Association Journal 25* (September, 1971): 25-36.

Madhubuti, Haki / Don L. Lee. *Black Men: Obsolete, Single Dangerous? The Afrikan Family in Transition.* Chicago: Third World Press, 1990.

—. *Black Pride.* Detroit: Broadside Press, 1968.

—. *Book of Life.* Chicago: Third World Press, 1973.

—. *Claiming Earth: Race Rage, Rape Redemption: Blacks Seeking a Culture of Enlightened Empowerment.* Chicago: Third World Press, 1994.

—. *Don't Cry, Scream.* Detroit: Broadside Press, 1969 (reissued by Third World Press).

—. *Directionscore: New and Selected Poems.* Detroit: Broadside Press, 1970.

—. *Dynamite Voices: Black Poets of the 1960's.* Detroit: Broadside Press, 1971.

—. *Earthquakes and Sunrise Missions: Poetry and Essays of Black Renewal.* Chicago: Third World Press, 1983.

—. *Enemies: The Clash of Races.* Chicago: Third World Press, 1978.

—. *From Plan to Planet: Life Studies: The Need for African Minds and Institutions.* Detroit: Broadside, Press and Chicago: Institute of Positive Education, 1973. (reissued by Third World Press).

—. *Groundwork: New and Selected Poems of Don L. Lee/Haki R. Madhubuti from 1966-1996.* Chicago: Third World Press, 1996.

—. *HeartLove: Wedding and Love Poems.* Chicago: Third World Press, 1998.

—. *Killing Memory, Seeking Ancestors.* Detroit: Lotus Press, 1987.

—. *Run Toward Fear: New Poems and a Poet's Handbook.* Chicago: Third World Press, 2004.

—. *Think Black!* Detroit: Broadside Press, 1967.

—. *Tough Notes: A Healing Call for Creating Exceptional Black Men.* Chicago: Third World Press, 2002.

—. *We Walk the Way of the New World.* Detroit: Broadside Press, 1970.

—. *Yellow Black: The First Twenty-one Years of a Poet's Life.* Chicago: Third World Press, 2005